FOOD I DIGITAL A

COOKBOOK

SIMPLE, EASY AND DELICIOUS RECIPES FOR DIGITAL AIR FRYER OVEN

HANNAH KENZIE

Table of Contents

Introduction

The Ninja Foodi Digital Air Fryer Oven is more than just an electric oven; it's a multi-purpose device that offers 8 different programmable cooking functions.

You can now say goodbye to your toaster, oven, fryer, because with this high technology device you won't need them anymore.

Are you still wondering if buy this fantastic product or not? I will help you by giving you 5 reasons why you want Ninja Foodi Digital Air Fryer Oven in your kitchen:

1. Healthier meals.

With this incredible cooking appliance you won't need to use much (or any) oil to get your food crispy and browned. This device is ideal for making fresh and frozen fries, onion rings, mozzarella sticks, chicken wings etc… You will finally enjoy your favourite food without getting concerned about your health.

2. Cook fast and efficiently.

It will take just 60 second to preheat and most of the heat stays inside. Food cooks faster than in the oven or the stove, because the heat is not lost in the surrounding air. Ninja Foodi Digital Air Fryer Oven won't heat up your house in the summer like all the traditional ovens, and the cost of the electricity used is just pennies.

3. Versatility.

As previously mentioned with this fantastic digital air fryer oven you can cook many different things in various ways. It really is more than just an oven!

4. Space – Saving.

When the oven is not in use, you can simply flip it up and away to store. You can get your counter space freed with just a flip.

5. Easy to use.

With Ninja Foodi Digital Air Fryer Oven, the only thing that you'll need to do is to put your food in the oven, set cooking function, the time and the temperature and then you will be free to walk away. It is so easy to use that you could teach your kids to use it for making after school snacks or quick lunches!

Ninja Foodi Digital Air Fryer Oven will revolutionize your way of cooking by saving time, money and space in your kitchen. Moreover, you will be always able to eat testy and healthy food anytime, anywhere.

The Ninja® Food i Digital Air Fry Oven

The Ninja Foodi Digital Air Fryer Oven is a smart cooking device that has revolutionized the way of cooking. This cooking appliance is a first of its kind type of Air Fry Oven from Ninja, which has features not found in other Air Fryer Ovens, together with its unique design.
When you will unbox the Ninja Foodi Digital Air Fryer Oven, you will find a rectangular unit with 19.7" width x 7.5" height x 15.1" depth. It contains a flip lid and control panel on the front. The Air Fryer basket, sheet pan, and crumb tray are removable, and they all are dishwasher safe.
The crumb tray is placed inside and at the bottom of the oven to prevent the food drippings from falling on the oven base. The sheet pan is used for baking, broiling, or toasting. Whereas the Air fryer basket is used to evenly air fry the food. The wire rack can also be used for roasting purposes.
The control panel has an LED screen on its top, and it shows the timer in hours and minutes; and temperature in Fahrenheit. This screen also lit "PRE" in red colour to show if the device is preheating and "HOT" to show if the appliance should be left for cooling. Once it cools down, the LED shows the "FLIP" sign to indicate that it is ready to be flipped in its vertical storage position.
The modes and functions of the oven are listed below the Led screen. By rotating the dial, the user can switch from one mode to another, and a blue light will appear on one side of the selected mode. The power key is used to switch on and off the device, whereas Temp and Time buttons are used to adjust the temperature and time as well to select the number of slices and darkness of the toasts while toasting.
There is a light bulb fixed inside the oven, which can be switch ON/OFF using the light button on the control panel. It will enable the users to check the doneness of the food while it is cooked inside.
This product is a revolutionary kitchen appliance, because it can be used in 8 different ways:

- Air fry
- Air roast
- Air broil
- Bake
- Dehydrate
- Keep warm
- Toast
- Bagel

One small device that contains all these functions will save you time, money and space in your kitchen. When you are done using it, you can easily store it away by just flipping it up against your backsplash, which it can be done very easily. With this multi-functional device you can get extra-large capacity without sacrificing counter space with its unique and modern design.

The Ninja Foodi Digital Air Fryer Oven it has become very popular thanks to its diverse benefits, which you will find listed below:

- Multi – purpose device - as I previously mentioned, this unique and small device can be used for air roasting, air frying, baking, toasting bread and bagel, broil food and dehydrate. You will able to do all this, just by pushing one button that will also give you the possibility to switch the cooking mode while using it.

- Flip up to store - unlike the others electric ovens, The Ninja Foodi Digital Air Fryer Oven can help you to spare some space in your kitchen when not in use. How? Just by simply flipping the oven up and away to store. By putting it vertically, you will get more space on your kitchen shelf. In fact it takes up 50% less space when you flip it up and away to store against your backsplash.

- Toaster function - yes, it an oven that works as a toaster as well. On the control panel you will find 2 options for toasting (bread and bagel): you will select "bagel" if you want to toast some bagels or simply "toast" if you want to toast some bread slices. You will be able to fit and toast up to 9 slices of bread at a time, in this way, no one will be waiting for their toasts to be done. Press the "time/slice" button and then turn the dial to choose the number of slices that you would like to toast. Press "temp/darkness" button and choose the level of darkness/lightness for your bread slices. You can get crispy dark brown, golden brown or even soft light brown toasts as you desire.

- Cook fast and evenly – its unique design promotes speed and even cooking results. One of the most interesting features is that it can preheat in 60 seconds and it cooks up to 60% faster than a traditional oven with Air Roast. Moreover, you will be able to cook family – sized meals in as little as 20 minutes. It does up to 40% more even baking compared to similar products. Capacity wise, The Ninja Foodi Digital Air Fryer Oven, has a 45% larger pan cooking area, compared to appliances with flat surface. You will be able to fit a 13-inch pizza, 9 slices of toasts and 6 chicken breasts (6-8 oz. each).

- Healthier food – whit the Air Frying function, you will get your food with 75% less fat compared to the traditional frying methods. This has been tested either for hand-cut and deep-fried French fries.

- Clean easily and efficiently – the cleaning and maintenance of this fantastic smart kitchen device is effortless. A removable back panel allows you to easily access the interior for deep cleaning. It won't be necessary to spend extra money in cleaning chemicals, but will be enough a cloth and a mild soapy water. In case you want to put the removable parts in the dishwasher, you can, because they are dishwasher safe.

- User-friendly – all the features, including the control panel, are very easy to understand and to use. All buttons are cleared marked for each and single function. The main dial will allows you to switch from one mode to another and to decrease or increase the temperature and the cooking time. You can press these same dial for pausing or starting a function. Moreover, in the display, will also appear when the device has completing the cooling down procedure and the oven is ready to be flipped up.

- High technology device – due to its Digital Crisp Control Technology, this smart appliance include a precision-controlled temperature, heat source and air flow for ultimate versatility and optimum cooking performance.

The Ninja Foodi Air Fry oven is easily on its online stores, and this countertop convection oven comes with following features and accessories:

- Ninja Air Fry Oven 1750-watt unit
- Wire rack (chrome plated)
- Sheet pan, 13x 13 inches, dishwasher safe
- Crumb tray (removable)
- Air fry basket, 13x 13 inches, dishwasher safe

Breakfast

AVOCADO TOAST

3 minutes	8 minutes	2

INGREDIENTS
4 bread slices
2 tablespoons butter, melted
1 avocado, peeled, pitted and cut into slices
A pinch of salt and black pepper
1 teaspoon oregano, dried
4 cheddar cheese slices

DIRECTIONS:

Spread the butter on each bread slice, divide the cheese, oregano and the avocado slices on 2 of them, top with the other 2 and cut each in halves. Arrange the sandwiches in your air fryer's basket and cook at 370 degrees f for 8 minutes.
Divide the sandwiches between plates and serve for breakfast.

NUTRITION:

Calories 189, Total Fat 11g, Saturated Fat 1.6g, Cholesterol 0mg, Sodium 439mg, Carbohydrates 20g, Fiber 5.4g, Sugars 1.8gProtein 3.8g

GREEN BEANS SALAD

10 minutes	15 minutes	4

INGREDIENTS
1-pound green beans, trimmed and halved
1 cup baby spinach
1 tablespoon balsamic vinegar
1 tablespoon olive oil
4 garlic cloves, minced
½ pound cherry tomatoes, halved
1 teaspoon chili powder
Salt and black pepper to the taste

DIRECTIONS:

Heat up your air fryer at 320 degrees f, add the oil, heat it up, add the green beans, garlic and the other ingredients, toss and cook for 15 minutes.
Divide the green beans mix into bowls and serve.

NUTRITION:

Calories 192, Total Fat 15g, Saturated Fat 4,8g, Cholesterol 22mg, Sodium 257mg, Carbohydrates 10g, Fiber 3.9g, Sugars 5g, Protein 7,2g

PEAS BAKE

5 minutes	20 minutes	4

INGREDIENTS

½ pound baby peas
1 tablespoon avocado oil
8 eggs, whisked
1 cup cheddar cheese, shredded
1 red onion, chopped
1 cup bacon, cooked and chopped
Salt and black pepper to the taste

DIRECTIONS:

Heat up the air fryer with the oil at 360 degrees f, add the onion and cook for 5 minutes.
Add the peas and the other ingredients except the cheese and toss.
Sprinkle the cheese on top, cook the mix for 15 minutes more, divide between plates and serve.

NUTRITION:

Calories 234, Total Fat 8g, Saturated Fat 2.6g, Cholesterol 0mg, Sodium 539mg, Carbohydrates 12g, Fiber 3,1g, Sugars 2gProtein 8g

CINNAMON APPLES OATMEAL

10 minutes	20 minutes	4

INGREDIENTS

2 cups coconut milk
1 cup steel cut oats
2 green apples, cored and cubed
1 teaspoon cinnamon powder
2 tablespoons brown sugar

DIRECTIONS:

In the air fryer's pan, combine the oats with the milk and the other ingredients, stir and cook at 360 degrees f for 17 minutes.
Divide into bowls and serve for breakfast.

NUTRITION:

Calories 157, Total Fat 2g, Saturated Fat 0.6g, Cholesterol 0mg, Sodium 200mg, Carbohydrates 33g, Fiber 3,6g, Sugars 12gProtein 3.8g

FRUIT BOWLS

DIRECTIONS:

In your air fryer's pan, combine the pear with the apple and the other ingredients, toss and cook at 360 degrees f for 10 minutes.
Divide into bowls and serve for breakfast.

NUTRITION:

Calories 62, Total Fat 1g, Saturated Fat 0,2g, Cholesterol 0mg, Sodium 10mg, Carbohydrates 15g, Fiber 2g, Sugars 2gProtein 1g

5 minutes	10 minutes	2

INGREDIENTS

1 cup heavy cream
1 tablespoon butter, soft
2 tablespoons sugar
½ cup walnuts, chopped
1 pear, cubed
1 apple, cored and cubed
1 mango, peeled and cubed
1 avocado, peeled and cubed

NUTS PUDDING

DIRECTIONS:

In your air fryer's pan, combine the coconut flakes with the nuts and the other ingredients, toss and cook at 360 degrees f for 20 minutes.
Divide into bowls and serve for breakfast.

NUTRITION:

Calories 136, Total Fat 0,5g, Saturated Fat 0,3g, Cholesterol 4mg, Sodium 297mg, Carbohydrates 20g, Fiber 1g, Sugars 6g, Protein 14g

5 minutes	20 minutes	4

INGREDIENTS

1 cup coconut flakes, unsweetened and shredded
1 cup almonds, chopped
½ cup walnuts, chopped
½ cup maple syrup
2 cups almond milk
½ cup heavy cream

RICE AND BERRIES PUDDING

5 minutes	20 minutes	4

INGREDIENTS

1 cup white rice
3 cups almond milk
1 cup blackberries
2 tablespoons sugar
2 tablespoons butter, soft
1 teaspoon vanilla extract

DIRECTIONS:

In your air fryer's pan, combine the rice with the almond milk and the other ingredients, toss and cook at 370 degrees f for 20 minutes.
Divide the rice pudding into bowls and serve.

NUTRITION:

Calories 153, Total Fat 2,2g, Saturated Fat 2g, Cholesterol 1,5mg, Sodium 39mg, Carbohydrates 31g, Fiber 1g, Sugars 17gProtein 3g

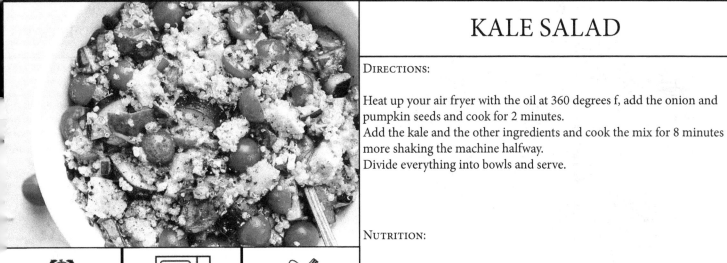

KALE SALAD

4 minutes	10 minutes	2

INGREDIENTS

1 tablespoon olive oil
3 cups kale, torn
1 red onion, chopped
A pinch of salt and black pepper
2 tablespoons pumpkin seeds
1 avocado, peeled, pitted and cubed
½ cup cherry tomatoes, halved
1 teaspoon oregano, dried

DIRECTIONS:

Heat up your air fryer with the oil at 360 degrees f, add the onion and pumpkin seeds and cook for 2 minutes.
Add the kale and the other ingredients and cook the mix for 8 minutes more shaking the machine halfway.
Divide everything into bowls and serve.

NUTRITION:

Calories 179, Total Fat 14g, Saturated Fat 2g, Cholesterol 0mg, Sodium 77mg, Carbohydrates 13g, Fiber 6g, Sugars 1gProtein 3.8g

CREAMY APPLES PUDDING

10 minutes	20 minutes	4

INGREDIENTS

1 cup brown rice
2 tablespoons sugar
2 cups coconut milk
½ teaspoon almond extract
1 cup apple, peeled, cored and chopped
Cooking spray

DIRECTIONS:

Grease your air fryer's pan with the cooking spray, combine the rice with the apples and the other ingredients inside, toss, cover and cook at 360 degrees f for 20 minutes, flipping it halfway.
Divide the pudding into bowls and serve for breakfast.

NUTRITION:

Calories 278, Total Fat 9g, Saturated Fat 5g, Cholesterol 22mg, Sodium 351mg, Carbohydrates 52g, Fiber 3g, Sugars 25gProtein 1g

PORK AND QUINOA MIX

5 minutes	20 minutes	4

INGREDIENTS

2 tablespoons olive oil
2 tablespoons lime juice
2 cups quinoa, cooked
1 pound pork stew meat, ground
8 ounces baby spinach, torn
1 red onion, chopped
1 teaspoon chili powder
A pinch of salt and black pepper

DIRECTIONS:

Heat up the air fryer with the oil at 360 degrees f, add the onion and chili powder and cook for 5 minutes.
Add the meat and cook for 5 minutes more.
Add the rest of the ingredients, toss, cook the mix for 10 minutes more, divide into bowls and serve.

NUTRITION:

Calories 336, Total Fat 23g, Saturated Fat 4,3g, Cholesterol 140mg, Sodium 497mg, Carbohydrates 26g, Fiber 4g, Sugars 4g, Protein 34g

BEANS AND EGGS MIX

10 minutes | 20 minutes | 4

INGREDIENTS
1 cup canned black beans, drained and rinsed
1 cup canned red kidney beans, drained and rinsed
1 red onion, chopped
2 tablespoons olive oil
8 eggs, whisked
Salt and black pepper to the taste
¼ cup mozzarella cheese, shredded
1 tablespoon chives, chopped

DIRECTIONS:

Grease your air fryer with the oil, heat it up at 380 degrees f, add the onion and the beans and cook for 5 minutes.
Add the eggs and the remaining ingredients, toss, cook for 15 minutes more, divide into bowls and serve.

NUTRITION:

Calories 213, Total Fat 8g, Saturated Fat 2g, Cholesterol 211mg, Sodium 100mg, Carbohydrates 26g, Fiber 9g, Sugars 1gProtein 15g

KALE CASSEROLE

10 minutes | 15 minutes | 4

INGREDIENTS
1 yellow onion, chopped
2 garlic cloves, minced
2 tablespoons olive oil
1 pound kale, torn
4 eggs, whisked
1 cup cheddar cheese, shredded
Salt and black pepper to the taste
1 teaspoon oregano, dried
½ teaspoon cumin, ground
1 tablespoon lemon juice

DIRECTIONS:

Heat up the air fryer with the oil at 370 degrees f, add the garlic and the onion and cook for 2 minutes.
Add the kale, eggs and the other ingredients except the cheese.
Sprinkle the cheese on top, cook the mix for 13 minutes more, divide between plates and serve.

NUTRITION:

Calories 229, Total Fat 14g, Saturated Fat 4g, Cholesterol 294mg, Sodium 277mg, Carbohydrates 6g, Fiber 2g, Sugars 3gProtein 20g

Appetizers & Snacks

SALMON PATTIES

DIRECTIONS:

Roll out puff pastry on a working surface, cut it in squares, divide the salmon, mozzarella and the other ingredients except the cooking spray on half of them, top with the other halves, seal the edges and grease the patties with the cooking spray.
Place all the patties in your air fryer's basket and cook at 370 degrees f for 12 minutes.
Divide the patties between plates and serve for breakfast.

5 minutes	12 minutes	4

NUTRITION:

Calories 250 , Total Fat 11g, Saturated Fat 3g, Cholesterol 155mg, Sodium 175mg, Carbohydrates 2g, Fiber 0g, Sugars 0g, Protein 30g

INGREDIENTS
1 puff pastry sheet
1 cup mozzarella, shredded
1 pound smoked salmon, skinless, boneless and flaked
½ cup tomatoes, cubed
A pinch of salt and black pepper
1 tablespoon chives, chopped
Cooking spray

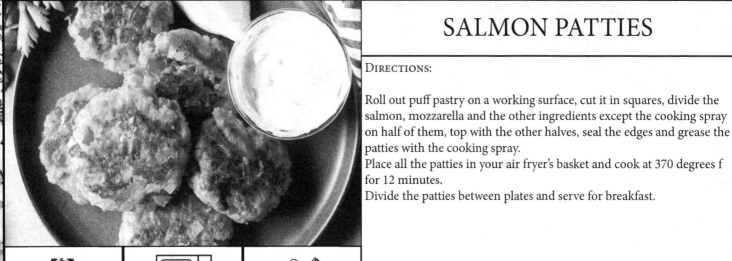

SALSA SHRIMP BOWLS

DIRECTIONS:

In your air fryer, combine the shrimp with the oil, chili and the other ingredients, toss and cook at 370 degrees f for 10 minutes shaking the machine halfway.
Divide the mix into bowls and serve for breakfast.

5 minutes	10 minutes	4

NUTRITION:

Calories 320, Total Fat 4g, Saturated Fat 1g, Cholesterol 194mg, Sodium 748mg, Carbohydrates 20g, Fiber 5g, Sugars 2gProtein 30g

INGREDIENTS
1 tablespoon olive oil
1 red chili, minced
1 red onion, chopped
1-pound shrimp, peeled and deveined
½ cup salsa
2 tablespoon parmesan, grated

CHICKEN BOWLS

6 minutes	20 minutes	4

Ingredients
8 eggs, whisked
1 pound chicken breast, skinless, boneless and cut into strips
1 tablespoon olive oil
1 yellow onion, chopped
1 teaspoon chili powder
1 cup baby spinach
1 tablespoon parsley, chopped
2 tablespoons chives, chopped
Salt and black pepper to the taste

Directions:

Heat up your air fryer with the oil at 360 degrees f, add the meat and onion and cook for 5 minutes.
Add the eggs mixed with the other ingredients, toss gently, cook for 15 minutes more, divide everything into bowls and serve for breakfast.

Nutrition:

Calories 378, Total Fat 10g, Saturated Fat 1g, Cholesterol 60mg, Sodium 250mg, Carbohydrates 45g, Fiber 7g, Sugars 3gProtein 27g

MAYO ZUCCHINI MIX

4 minutes	10 minutes	4

Ingredients
1 tablespoon avocado oil
1 pound zucchinis, roughly cubed
1 yellow onion, chopped
1 teaspoon turmeric powder
1 cup baby kale
2 tablespoons mayonnaise
2 tablespoons mustard
1 cup parmesan cheese, grated

Directions:

Heat up the air fryer with the oil at 360 degrees f, add the onion, zucchinis and turmeric and cook for 2 minutes.
Add the other ingredients, toss, cook for 8 minutes more, divide between plates and serve for breakfast right away.

Nutrition:

Calories 106, Total Fat 10g, Saturated Fat 2g, Cholesterol 30mg, Sodium 97mg, Carbohydrates 1g, Fiber 1g, Sugars 1g, Protein 1g

AIR FRIED CHURROS

10 minutes	12 minutes	6

INGREDIENTS
1 cup of water
1/3 cup butter, cut into cubes
2 tbsp granulated sugar
1/4 tsp salt
1 cup flour, preferably all-purpose
2 large eggs
1 tsp vanilla extract
oil spray

Cinnamon Coating:
1/2 cup granulated sugar
3/4 tsp ground cinnamon

DIRECTIONS:

Grease the Ninja baking pan with cooking spray.
Warm water with butter, salt, and sugar in a saucepan until it boils.
Now reduce its heat then slowly stir in flour and mix well until smooth.
Remove the mixture from the heat and leave it for 4 minutes to cool.
Add vanilla extract and eggs, then beat the mixture until it comes together as a batter.
Transfer this churro mixture to a piping bag with star-shaped tips and pipe the batter on the prepared pan to get 4-inch churros using this batter.
Refrigerate these churros for 1 hour then transfer them to the Air fry sheet.
Place the churros to the Ninja oven and Close its lid.
Rotate the Ninja Foodi dial to select the "Air Fry" mode.
Press the Time button and again use the dial to set the cooking time to 12 minutes.
Now press the Temp button and rotate the dial to set the temperature at 375 degrees F.
Meanwhile, mix granulated sugar with cinnamon in a bowl.
Drizzle this mixture over the air fried churros.
Serve.

NUTRITION:

Calories 176, Total Fat 10g, Saturated Fat 5g, Cholesterol 84mg, Sodium 115mg, Carbohydrates 17g, Fiber 0,5g, Sugars 10gProtein 4g

AIR FRIED DOUGHNUTS

10 minutes	14 minutes	6

INGREDIENTS
Cooking spray
1/2 cup milk
1/4 cup 1 tsp granulated sugar
2 1/4 tsp active dry yeast
2 cup flour, preferably all-purpose
1/2 tsp Salt
4 tbsp melted butter
1 large egg
1 tsp pure vanilla extract

DIRECTIONS:

Warm up the milk in a saucepan then add yeast and 1 tsp sugar.
Mix well and leave this milk for 8 minutes.
Add flour, salt, butter, egg, vanilla, and ¼ cup sugar to the warm milk.
Mix well and knead over a floured surface until smooth.
Place this doughnut dough in a lightly greased bowl and brush it with cooking oil.
Cover the dough and leave it at a warm place for 1 hour.
Punch the raised dough then roll into ½ inch thick rectangle.
Cut 3" circles out of this dough sheet using a biscuit cutter.
Now cut the rounds from the center to make a hole.
Place these doughnuts on the Air Fryer.
Transfer these doughnuts to the Ninja oven and Close its lid.
Rotate the Ninja Foodi dial to select the "Air Fry" mode.
Press the Time button and again use the dial to set the cooking time to 6 minutes.
Now press the Temp button and rotate the dial to set the temperature at 375 degrees F.
Cook the doughnuts in batches to avoid overcrowding.
Serve fresh.

NUTRITION:

Calories 269, Total Fat 10g, Saturated Fat 4g, Cholesterol 67mg, Sodium 390mg, Carbohydrates 43g, Fiber 1g, Sugars 18gProtein 4g

MOLTEN LAVA CAKES

Prep time	Cook time	Servings
10 minutes	13 minutes	4

INGREDIENTS

1 ½ tbsp self-rising flour
3 ½ tbsp baker's sugar
3 ½ oz. unsalted butter
3 ½ oz. dark chocolate, chopped
2 eggs

DIRECTIONS:

Grease 4 ramekins with cooking spray and keep them aside.
First, melt the butter with dark chocolate in a glass bowl by heating in the microwave for 3 minutes.
Beat eggs with sugar in a mixer until fluffy and pale.
Stir in melted chocolate, and flour then mix well until smooth.
Divide the chocolate batter in the ramekins and place these ramekins in the Ninja oven.
Seal the Ninja oven by closing its lid.
Rotate the Ninja Foodi dial to select the "Air Fry" mode.
Press the Time button and again use the dial to set the cooking time to 10 minutes.
Now press the Temp button and rotate the dial to set the temperature at 375 degrees F.
Serve.

NUTRITION:

Calories 425, Total Fat 38g, Saturated Fat 22g, Cholesterol 214mg, Sodium 50mg, Carbohydrates 21g, Fiber 4g, Sugars 12gProtein 7g

FRIED OREOS

Prep time	Cook time	Servings
10 minutes	4 minutes	4

INGREDIENTS

1 crescent sheet roll
9 Oreo cookies

DIRECTIONS:

Spread the crescent sheet roll and cut it into 9 squares of equal size.
Place one oreo cookie at the center of each square and wrap the crescent sheets around the cookies.
Place these wrapped cookies in the Air Fryer.
Transfer the cookies to the Ninja oven and Close its lid.
Rotate the Ninja Foodi dial to select the "Air Fry" mode.
Press the Time button and again use the dial to set the cooking time to 4 minutes.
Now press the Temp button and rotate the dial to set the temperature at 360 degrees F.
Serve fresh.

NUTRITION:

Calories 106, Total Fat 6g, Saturated Fat 1g, Cholesterol 8mg, Sodium 130mg, Carbohydrates 11g, Fiber 1g, Sugars 5g, Protein 1g

CHOCOLATE CHIP COOKIE

10 minutes	12 minutes	6

INGREDIENTS

1/2 cup butter, softened
1/2 cup sugar
1/2 cup brown sugar
1 egg
1 tsp vanilla
1/2 tsp baking soda
1/4 tsp salt
1 1/2 cups flour, preferably all-purpose
1 cup of chocolate chips

DIRECTIONS:

Grease the Ninja baking pan with cooking spray.
Beat butter with sugar and brown sugar in a mixing bowl.
Stir in vanilla, egg, salt, flour, and baking soda, then mix well.
Fold in chocolate chips then knead this dough a bit.
Spread the dough in the prepared baking pan evenly.
Transfer this pan to the Ninja oven and Close its lid.
Rotate the Ninja Foodi dial to select the "Bake" mode.
Press the Time button and again use the dial to set the cooking time to 12 minutes.
Now press the Temp button and rotate the dial to set the temperature at 400 degrees F.
Serve oven fresh.

NUTRITION:

Calories 120, Total Fat 4g, Saturated Fat 2g, Cholesterol 8mg, Sodium 64mg, Carbohydrates 22g, Fiber 0g, Sugars 14g, Protein 1g

BLUEBERRY HAND PIES

10 minutes	25 minutes	6

NGREDIENTS

. cup blueberries
.5 tbsp caster sugar
tsp lemon juice
pinch salt
4 oz. refrigerated pie crust
vater
anilla sugar to sprinkle on top

DIRECTIONS:

Toss the blueberries with salt, lemon juice, and sugar in a medium bowl.
Spread the pie crust into a round sheet and cut 6-4 inch circles out of it.
Add a tbsp of blueberry filling at the center of each circle.
Moisten the edges of these circles and fold them in half then pinch their edges together.
Press the edges using a fork to crimp its edges.
Place the handpieces in the Air Fryer and spray them with cooking oil.
Drizzle the vanilla sugar over the hand pies.
Transfer the hand pies on the Air Fryer to the Ninja oven and Close its lid.
Rotate the Ninja Foodi dial to select the "Air Fry" mode.
Press the Time button and again use the dial to set the cooking time to 25 minutes.
Now press the Temp button and rotate the dial to set the temperature at 400 degrees F.
Serve fresh.

NUTRITION:

Calories 247, Total Fat 16g, Saturated Fat 10g, Cholesterol 27mg, Sodium 92mg, Carbohydrates 36g, Fiber 3g, Sugars 13g, Protein 4g

CHERRY JAM TARTS

10 minutes	40 minutes	12

INGREDIENTS
2 sheets shortcrust pastry
For the frangipane
4 oz. butter softened
4 oz. golden caster sugar
1 egg
1 tbsp plain flour
4 oz. ground almonds
3 oz. cherry jam
For the icing
1 cup icing sugar
12 glacé cherries

DIRECTIONS:
Grease the 12 cups of the muffin tray with butter.
Roll the puff pastry into a 10 cm sheet then cut 12 rounds out of it.
Place these rounds into each muffin cups and press them into these cups.
Transfer the muffin tray to the refrigerator and leave it for 20 minutes.
Add dried beans or pulses into each tart crust to add weight.
Transfer the muffin tray to the Ninja oven and Close its lid.
Rotate the Ninja Foodi dial to select the "Bake" mode.
Press the Time button and again use the dial to set the cooking time to 10 minutes.
Now press the Temp button and rotate the dial to set the temperature at 350 degrees F.
Now remove the dried beans from the crust and bake again for 10 minutes in the Ninja oven.
Meanwhile, prepare the filling beat beating butter with sugar and egg until fluffy.
Stir in flour and almonds ground then mix well.
Divide this filling in the baked crusts and top them with a tbsp cherry jam.
Now again, place the muffin tray in the Ninja oven.
Continue cooking on the "Bake" mode for 20 minutes at 350 degrees F.
Whisk the icing sugar with 2 tbsp water and top the baked tarts with sugar mixture.

NUTRITION:

Calories 91, Total Fat 0,2g, Saturated Fat 0,1g, Cholesterol 0mg, Sodium 114mg, Carbohydrates 21g, Fiber 0g, Sugars 8gProtein 1g

BROWNIE BARS

10 minutes	28 minutes	8

INGREDIENTS
Brownie:
1/2 cup butter, cubed
1-oz. unsweetened chocolate
2 large eggs, beaten
1 tsp vanilla extract
1 cup of sugar
1 cup flour, preferably all-purpose
1 tsp baking powder
1 cup walnuts, chopped

Filling:
6 oz. cream cheese softened
1/2 cup sugar
1/4 cup butter, softened
2 tbsp all-purpose flour
1 large egg, beaten
1/2 tsp vanilla extract

Topping:
1 cup (6 oz.) chocolate chips
1 cup walnuts, chopped
2 cups mini marshmallows

Frosting:
1/4 cup butter
1/4 cup milk
2 oz. cream cheese
1-oz. unsweetened chocolate
3 cups confectioners' sugar
1 tsp vanilla extract

DIRECTIONS:

In a small bowl, add and whisk all the ingredients for filling until smooth.
Melt butter with chocolate in a large saucepan over medium heat.
Mix well, then remove the melted chocolate from the heat.
Now stir in vanilla, eggs, baking powder, flour, sugar, and nuts then mix well.
Spread this chocolate batter in the Ninja baking pan.
Drizzle nuts, marshmallows, and chocolate chips over the batter.
Place this baking pan in the Ninja oven and Close its lid.
Rotate the Ninja Foodi dial to select the "Air Fry" mode.
Press the Time button and again use the dial to set the cooking time to 28 minutes.
Now press the Temp button and rotate the dial to set the temperature at 350 degrees F.
Meanwhile, prepare the frosting by heating butter with cream cheese, chocolate and milk in a saucepan over medium heat.
Mix well, then remove it from the heat.
Stir in vanilla and sugar, then mix well.
Pour this frosting over the brownie.
Allow the brownie to cool then slice into bars.

NUTRITION:
Calories 106, Total Fat 6g, Saturated Fat 1g, Cholesterol 8mg, Sodium 130mg, Carbohydrates 11g, Fiber 1g, Sugars 5g, Protein 1g

Vegetarian

MOM'S VEGGIE FRITTERS

30 minutes	15 minutes	3

INGREDIENTS
1 cup celery, chopped
1 cup cauliflower rice
2 garlic cloves, minced
1 shallot, chopped
Sea salt and ground black pepper, to taste
2 tablespoons fresh parsley, chopped
1 egg, well beaten
1 cup romano cheese, grated
1/2 cup almond flour
1 tablespoon olive oil

DIRECTIONS:

Mix the veggies, spices, egg, almond flour, and romano cheese until everything is well incorporated.
Take 1 tablespoon of the veggie mixture and roll into a ball. Roll the balls onto the dried bread flakes. Brush the veggie balls with olive oil on all sides.
Cook in the preheated air fryer at 360 degrees f for 15 minutes or until thoroughly cooked and crispy.
Repeat the process until you run out of ingredients and serve.

NUTRITION:

Calories 98, Total Fat 2g, Saturated Fat 0,5g, Cholesterol 57mg, Sodium 61mg, Carbohydrates 17g, Fiber 2g, Sugars 1gProtein 4g

FRIED PICKLES WITH DIJON SAUCE

15 minutes	10 minutes	2

INGREDIENTS
1 egg, whisked
2 tablespoons buttermilk
1/2 cup romano cheese, grated
1/2 teaspoon onion powder
1/2 teaspoon garlic powder
1 ½ cups dill pickle chips, pressed dry with kitchen towels
Mayo sauce:
1/3 cup mayonnaise
1 tablespoon dijon mustard
1 tablespoon ketchup
1/4 teaspoon ground black pepper

DIRECTIONS:

In a shallow bowl, whisk the egg with buttermilk.
In another bowl, mix romano cheese, onion powder, and garlic powder.
Dredge the pickle chips in the egg mixture, then, in the cheese mixture.
Cook in the preheated air fryer at 400 degrees f for 5 minutes; shake the basket and cook for 5 minutes more.
Meanwhile, mix all the sauce ingredients until well combined. Serve the fried pickles with the mayo sauce for dipping.

NUTRITION:

Calories 94, Total Fat 0,8g, Saturated Fat 0,3g, Cholesterol 11mg, Sodium 870mg, Carbohydrates 18g, Fiber 1g, Sugars 2g, Protein 3g

CRISPY GREEN BEANS WITH PECORINO ROMANO

15 minutes	7 minutes	3

INGREDIENTS

2 tablespoons buttermilk
1 egg
4 tablespoons almond meal
4 tablespoons golden flaxseed meal
4 tablespoons pecorino romano cheese, finely grated
Coarse salt and crushed black pepper, to taste
1 teaspoon smoked paprika
6 ounces green beans, trimmed

DIRECTIONS:

In a shallow bowl, whisk together the buttermilk and egg.
In a separate bowl, combine the almond meal, golden flaxseed meal, pecorino romano cheese, salt, black pepper, and paprika.
Dip the green beans in the egg mixture, then, in the cheese mixture.
Place the green beans in the lightly greased cooking basket.
Cook in the preheated air fryer at 390 degrees f for 4 minutes. Shake the basket and cook for a further 3 minutes.
Taste, adjust the seasonings, and serve with the dipping sauce if desired.

NUTRITION:

Calories 201, Total Fat 20g, Saturated Fat 6g, Cholesterol 80mg, Sodium 364mg, Carbohydrates 29g, Fiber 10g, Sugars 8g, Protein 9g

SPICY CELERY STICKS

20 minutes	15 minutes	4

NGREDIENTS

pound celery, cut into matchticks
: tablespoons peanut oil
jalapeño, seeded and minced
/4 teaspoon dill
/2 teaspoon basil
alt and white pepper to taste

DIRECTIONS:

Start by preheating your air fryer to 380 degrees f.
Toss all ingredients together and place them in the air fryer basket.
Cook for 15 minutes, shaking the basket halfway through the cooking time. Transfer to a serving platter and enjoy!

NUTRITION:

Calories 37, Total Fat 1g, Saturated Fat 0,2g, Cholesterol 2mg, Sodium 160mg, Carbohydrates 3g, Fiber 0g, Sugars 0g, Protein 4g

THE BEST AVOCADO FRIES EVER

50 minutes	45 minutes	4

INGREDIENTS
1/2 head garlic (6-7 cloves
1/2 cup almond meal
Sea salt and ground black pepper, to taste
2 eggs
1/2 cup parmesan cheese, grated
2 avocados, cut into wedges

Sauce:
1/2 cup mayonnaise
1 teaspoon lemon juice
1 teaspoon mustard

DIRECTIONS:

Place the garlic on a piece of aluminum foil and spritz with cooking spray. Wrap the garlic in the foil.
Cook in the preheated air fryer at 400 degrees for 12 minutes. Check the garlic, open the top of the foil and continue to cook for 10 minutes more.
Let it cool for 10 to 15 minutes; remove the cloves by squeezing them out of the skins; mash the garlic and reserve.
In a shallow bowl, combine the almond meal, salt, and black pepper. In another shallow dish, whisk the eggs until frothy.
Place the parmesan cheese in a third shallow dish. Dredge the avocado wedges in the almond meal mixture, shaking off the excess. Then, dip in the egg mixture; lastly, dredge in parmesan cheese.
Spritz the avocado wedges with cooking oil on all sides.
Cook in the preheated air fryer at 395 degrees f approximately 8 minutes, turning them over halfway through the cooking time.
Meanwhile, combine the sauce ingredients with the smashed roasted garlic. To serve, divide the avocado fries between plates and top with the sauce.

NUTRITION:

Calories 40, Total Fat 3g, Saturated Fat 0,8g, Cholesterol 0mg, Sodium 104mg, Carbohydrates 2,4g, Fiber 1,6g, Sugars 0,4gProtein 0,4g

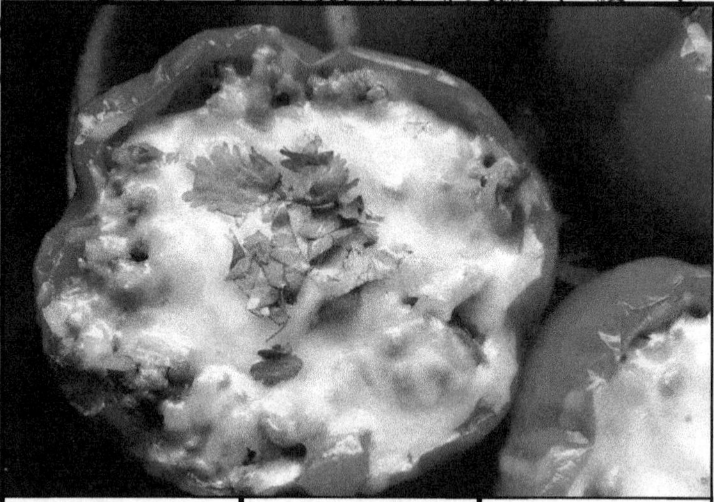

COTTAGE AND MAYONNAISE STUFFED PEPPERS

20 minutes	15 minutes	2

INGREDIENTS
1 red bell pepper, top and seeds removed
1 yellow bell pepper, top and seeds removed
Salt and pepper, to taste
1 cup cottage cheese
4 tablespoons mayonnaise
2 pickles, chopped

DIRECTIONS:

Arrange the peppers in the lightly greased cooking basket. Cook in the preheated air fryer at 400 degrees f for 15 minutes, turning them over halfway through the cooking time.
Season with salt and pepper.
Then, in a mixing bowl, combine the cream cheese with the mayonnaise and chopped pickles. Stuff the pepper with the cream cheese mixture and serve.

NUTRITION:

Calories 164, Total Fat 12g, Saturated Fat 4,3g, Cholesterol 31mg, Sodium 150mg, Carbohydrates 5g, Fiber 1g, Sugars 2g, Protein 8g

STUFFED MUSHROOMS WITH CHEESE AND HERBS

15 minutes	7 minutes	3

INGREDIENTS

9 large button mushrooms, stems removed
1 tablespoon olive oil
Salt and ground black pepper, to taste
1/2 teaspoon dried rosemary
6 tablespoons swiss cheese shredded
6 tablespoons romano cheese, shredded
6 tablespoons cream cheese
1 teaspoon soy sauce
1 teaspoon garlic, minced
3 tablespoons green onions, minced

DIRECTIONS:

Brush the mushroom caps with olive oil; sprinkle with salt, pepper, and rosemary.
In a mixing bowl, thoroughly combine the remaining ingredients; mix to combine well and divide the filling mixture among the mushroom caps.
Cook in the preheated air fryer at 390 degrees f for 7 minutes.
Let the mushrooms cool slightly before serving.

NUTRITION:

Calories 71, Total Fat 2g, Saturated Fat 1g, Cholesterol 4mg, Sodium 464mg, Carbohydrates 8g, Fiber 2g, Sugars 2g, Protein 6g

MEDITERRANEAN VEGETABLE GRATIN

35 minutes	25 minutes	4

INGREDIENTS

1 eggplant, peeled and sliced
2 bell peppers, seeded and sliced
1 red onion, sliced
1 teaspoon fresh garlic, minced
4 tablespoons olive oil
1 teaspoon mustard
1 teaspoon dried oregano
1 teaspoon smoked paprika
Salt and ground black pepper, to taste
1 tomato, sliced
6 ounces halloumi cheese, sliced lengthways

DIRECTIONS:

Start by preheating your air fryer to 370 degrees f. Spritz a baking pan with nonstick cooking spray.
Place the eggplant, peppers, onion, and garlic on the bottom of the baking pan. Add the olive oil, mustard, and spices. Transfer to the cooking basket and cook for 14 minutes.
Top with the tomatoes and cheese; increase the temperature to 390 degrees f and cook for 5 minutes more until bubbling. Let it sit on a cooling rack for 10 minutes before serving.

NUTRITION:

Calories 207, Total Fat 20g, Saturated Fat 3g, Cholesterol 1mg, Sodium 90mg, Carbohydrates 8g, Fiber 2g, Sugars 3g, Protein 2g

CHINESE CABBAGE BAKE

35 minutes	30 minutes	4

Ingredients

1/2 pound chinese cabbage, roughly chopped
2 bell peppers, seeded and sliced
1 jalapeno pepper, seeded and sliced
1 onion, thickly sliced
2 garlic cloves, sliced
1/2 stick butter
4 tablespoons flaxseed meal
1/2 cup milk
1 cup cream cheese
Sea salt and freshly ground black pepper, to taste
1/2 teaspoon cayenne pepper
1 cup monterey jack cheese, shredded

Directions:

Heat a pan of salted water and bring to a boil. Boil the chinese cabbage for 2 to 3 minutes. Transfer the chinese cabbage to cold water to stop the cooking process.
Place the chinese cabbage in a lightly greased casserole dish. Add the peppers, onion, and garlic.
Next, melt the butter in a saucepan over a moderate heat. Gradually add the flaxseed meal and cook for 2 minutes to form a paste.
Slowly pour in the milk, stirring continuously until a thick sauce forms. Add the cream cheese. Season with the salt, black pepper, and cayenne pepper. Add the mixture to the casserole dish.
Top with the shredded monterey jack cheese and bake in the preheated air fryer at 390 degrees f for 25 minutes. Serve hot.

Nutrition:

Calories 127, Total Fat 9g, Saturated Fat 1g, Cholesterol 1mg, Sodium 191mg, Carbohydrates 11g, Fiber 1g, Sugars 6gProtein 1g

CRISPY LEEK STRIPS

52 minutes	43 minutes	6

Ingredients

1/2 teaspoon porcini powder
1 cup almond flour
1/2 cup coconut flour
1 tablespoon vegetable oil
2 medium-sized leeks, slice into julienne strips
2 large-sized dishes with ice water
2 teaspoons onion powder
Fine sea salt and cayenne pepper, to taste

Directions:

Allow the leeks to soak in ice water for about 25 minutes; drain well.
Place the flour, salt, cayenne pepper, onions powder, and porcini powder into a resealable bag. Add the leeks and shake to coat well.
Drizzle vegetable oil over the seasoned leeks. Air fry at 390 degrees f for about 18 minutes; turn them halfway through the cooking time.
Serve with homemade mayonnaise or any other sauce for dipping.

Nutrition:

Calories 114, Total Fat 9g, Saturated Fat 4g, Cholesterol 81mg, Sodium 120mg, Carbohydrates 3g, Fiber 2g, Sugars 2g, Protein 3g

MUSHROOMS WITH TAHINI SAUCE

22 minutes	19 minutes	5

INGREDIENTS
1/2 cup tahini
1/2 teaspoon turmeric powder
1/3 teaspoon cayenne pepper
2 tablespoons lemon juice, freshly squeezed
1 teaspoon kosher salt
1/3 teaspoon freshly cracked black pepper
1 1/2 tablespoons vermouth
1 ½ tablespoons olive oil
1 ½ pounds cremini mushrooms

DIRECTIONS:

Grab a mixing dish and toss the mushrooms with the olive oil, turmeric powder, salt, black pepper, and cayenne pepper.
Cook them in your air fryer for 9 minutes at 355 degrees f.
Pause your air fryer, give it a good stir and cook for 10 minutes longer.
Meanwhile, thoroughly combine lemon juice, vermouth, and tahini.
Serve warm mushrooms with tahini sauce.

NUTRITION:

Calories 211, Total Fat 17g, Saturated Fat 5g, Cholesterol 89mg, Sodium 364mg, Carbohydrates 4g, Fiber 1g, Sugars 1g, Protein 3g

KETO CAULIFLOWER HASH BROWNS

23 minutes	17 minutes	6

NGREDIENTS
/2 cup cheddar cheese, shredded
tablespoon soft cheese, at room emperature
/3 cup almond meal
½ yellow or white medium-sized nion, chopped
ounces condensed cream of celery oup
tablespoon fresh cilantro, finely minced
1/3 cup sour cream
3 cloves garlic, peeled and finely minced
2 cups cauliflower, grated
1 1/2 tablespoons margarine, melted
Sea salt and freshly ground black pepper, to your liking
Crushed red pepper flakes, to your liking

DIRECTIONS:

Grab a large-sized bowl and whisk the celery soup, sour cream, soft cheese, red pepper, salt, and black pepper. Stir in the cauliflower, onion, garlic, cilantro, and cheddar cheese. Mix until everything is thoroughly combined.
Scrape the mixture into a baking dish that is previously lightly greased.
In another mixing bowl, combine together the almond meal and melted margarine. Spread the mixture evenly over the top of the hash brown mixture.
Bake for 17 minutes at 290 degrees f. Eat warm, garnished with some extra sour cream if desired.

NUTRITION:

Calories 117, Total Fat 8g, Saturated Fat 4g, Cholesterol 54mg, Sodium 484mg, Carbohydrates 3g, Fiber 2g, Sugars 1g, Protein 9g

SPICY RICOTTA STUFFED MUSHROOMS

DIRECTIONS:

Remove the stems from the mushroom caps and chop them; mix the chopped mushrooms steams with the salt, black pepper, cheese, chili powder, and paprika.
Add in eggs and mix to combine well. Stuff the mushroom caps with the egg/cheese filling.
To with parmesan cheese. Spritz the stuffed mushrooms with cooking spray.
Cook in the preheated air fryer at 360 degrees f for 18 minutes.

NUTRITION:

Calories 200, Total Fat 9g, Saturated Fat 5g, Cholesterol 66mg, Sodium 717mg, Carbohydrates 15g, Fiber 2g, Sugars 6g,Protein 15g

🕐 25 minutes	📺 18 minutes	🍴 4

INGREDIENTS
1 pound small white mushrooms
Sea salt and ground black pepper, to taste
4 tablespoons ricotta cheese
1/2 teaspoon ancho chili powder
1 teaspoon paprika
1 egg
1/2 cup parmesan cheese, grated

CAULIFLOWER WITH CHOLULA SAUCE

DIRECTIONS:

Start by preheating your air fryer to 400 degrees f. Lightly grease a baking pan with cooking spray.
In a mixing bowl, combine the almond flour, flaxseed meal, water, spices, and olive oil. Coat the cauliflower with the prepared batter; arrange the cauliflower on the baking pan.
Then, bake in the preheated air fryer for 8 minutes or until golden brown.
Brush the cholula sauce all over the cauliflower florets and bake an additional 4 to 5 minutes.

NUTRITION:

Calories 240, Total Fat 6g, Saturated Fat 1g, Cholesterol 0mg, Sodium 1012mg, Carbohydrates 37g, Fiber 6g, Sugars 2g, Protein 8g

🕐 20 minutes	📺 13 minutes	🍴 4

INGREDIENTS
1/2 cup almond flour
2 tablespoons flaxseed meal
1/2 cup water
Salt, to taste
1/2 teaspoon ground black pepper
1/2 teaspoon shallot powder
1/2 teaspoon garlic powder
1/2 teaspoon cayenne pepper
2 tablespoons olive oil
1 pound cauliflower, broken into small florets
1/4 cup cholula sauce

CELERIAC WITH GREEK YOGURT DIP

DIRECTIONS:

Place the vegetables in a single layer in the lightly greased cooking basket. Drizzle the sesame oil over vegetables.
Sprinkle with black pepper and sea salt.
Cook at 390 degrees f for 20 minutes, shaking the basket halfway through the cooking time.
Meanwhile, make the sauce by whisking all ingredients. Spoon the sauce over the roasted vegetables.

25 minutes	20 minutes	2

INGREDIENTS
1/2 pound celeriac, cut into 1 1/2-inch pieces
1 red onion, cut into 1 1/2-inch pieces
1 tablespoon sesame oil
1/2 teaspoon ground black pepper, to taste
1/2 teaspoon sea salt

Spiced yogurt:
1/4 cup greek yogurt
2 tablespoons mayonnaise
1/2 teaspoon mustard seeds
1/2 teaspoon chili powder

NUTRITION:

Calories 173, Total Fat 10g, Saturated Fat 1g, Cholesterol 4mg, Sodium 360mg, Carbohydrates 16g, Fiber 3g, Sugars 4g, Protein 4g

TANGY ASPARAGUS AND BROCCOLI

DIRECTIONS:

Place the vegetables in a single layer in the lightly greased cooking basket. Drizzle the peanut oil over the vegetables.
Sprinkle with salt and white pepper.
Cook at 380 degrees f for 15 minutes, shaking the basket halfway through the cooking time.
Add 1/2 cup of chicken broth to a saucepan; bring to a rapid boil and add the vinegar. Cook for 5 to 7 minutes or until the sauce has reduced by half.
Spoon the sauce over the warm vegetables and serve immediately.

25 minutes	20 minutes	4

INGREDIENTS
1/2 pound asparagus, cut into 1 1/2-inch pieces
1/2 pound broccoli, cut into 1 1/2-inch pieces
2 tablespoons peanut oil
Some salt and white pepper, to taste
1/2 cup chicken broth
2 tablespoons apple cider vinegar

NUTRITION:

Calories 87, Total Fat 3g, Saturated Fat 0,4g, Cholesterol 0mg, Sodium 48mg, Carbohydrates 11g, Fiber 6g, Sugars 1g, Protein 7g

COLORFUL VEGETABLE CROQUETTES

40 minutes	35 minutes	4

Ingredients

- 1/2 pound broccoli
- 4 tablespoons milk
- 2 tablespoons butter
- Salt and black pepper, to taste
- 1/2 teaspoon cayenne pepper
- 1/2 cup mushrooms, chopped
- 1 bell pepper, chopped
- 1 clove garlic, minced
- 3 tablespoons scallions, minced
- 2 tablespoons olive oil
- 1/2 cup almond flour
- 1/4 cup coconut flour
- 2 eggs
- 1/2 cup parmesan cheese, grated

Directions:

In a large saucepan, boil the broccoli for 17 to 20 minutes. Drain the broccoli and mash with the milk, butter, salt, black pepper, and cayenne pepper.
Add the mushrooms, bell pepper, garlic, scallions, and olive oil; stir to combine well. Shape the mixture into patties.
In a shallow bowl, place the flour; beat the eggs in another bowl; in a third bowl, place the parmesan cheese.
Dip each patty into the flour, followed by the eggs, and then the parmesan cheese; press to adhere.
Cook in the preheated air fryer at 375 degrees f for 16 minutes, shaking halfway through the cooking time.

Nutrition:

Calories 280, Total Fat 22g, Saturated Fat 6g, Cholesterol 86mg, Sodium 417mg, Carbohydrates 10g, Fiber 3g, Sugars 2g,Protein 6g

CAULIFLOWER WITH CHOLULA SAUCE

40 minutes	35 minutes	6

Ingredients

- 1 tablespoon olive oil
- 1 shallot, sliced
- 2 cloves garlic, minced
- 1 red bell pepper, seeded and sliced
- 1 yellow bell pepper, seeded and sliced
- 1 ½ cups kale
- 1 pound broccoli florets, steamed
- 6 eggs
- 1/2 cup milk
- Sea salt and ground black pepper, to your liking
- 1 cup swiss cheese, shredded
- 4 tablespoons romano cheese, grated

Directions:

Heat the olive oil in a saucepan over medium-high heat. Sauté the shallot, garlic, and peppers for 2 to 3 minutes. Add the kale and cook until wilted.
Arrange the broccoli florets evenly over the bottom of a lightly greased casserole dish. Spread the sautéed mixture over the top.
In a mixing bowl, thoroughly combine the eggs, milk, salt, pepper, and shredded cheese. Pour the mixture into the casserole dish.
Lastly, top with romano cheese. Bake at 330 degrees f for 30 minutes or until top is golden brown.

Nutrition:

Calories 212, Total Fat 14g, Saturated Fat 4g, Cholesterol 50mg, Sodium 301mg, Carbohydrates 10g, Fiber 6g, Sugars 3g, Protein 14g

Fish And Seafood

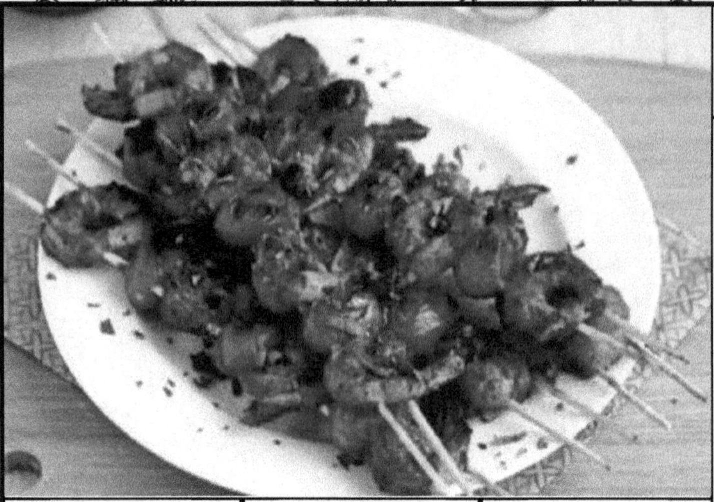

SPICY SHRIMP KEBAB

25 minutes	20 minutes	4

INGREDIENTS

- 1 ½ pounds jumbo shrimp, cleaned, shelled and deveined
- 1 pound cherry tomatoes
- 2 tablespoons butter, melted
- 1 tablespoons sriracha sauce
- Sea salt and ground black pepper, to taste
- 1/2 teaspoon dried oregano
- 1/2 teaspoon dried basil
- 1 teaspoon dried parsley flakes
- 1/2 teaspoon marjoram
- 1/2 teaspoon mustard seeds

DIRECTIONS:

Toss all ingredients in a mixing bowl until the shrimp and tomatoes are covered on all sides.
Soak the wooden skewers in water for 15 minutes.
Thread the jumbo shrimp and cherry tomatoes onto skewers. Cook in the preheated air fryer at 400 degrees f for 5 minutes, working with batches.

NUTRITION:

Calories 142, Total Fat 3,5g, Saturated Fat 0,7g, Cholesterol 146mg, Sodium 255mg, Carbohydrates 5,7g, Fiber 1g, Sugars 1g,Protein 20g

CRUMBED FISH FILLETS WITH TARRAGON

25 minutes	20 minutes	4

INGREDIENTS

- 2 eggs, beaten
- 1/2 teaspoon tarragon
- 4 fish fillets, halved
- 2 tablespoons dry white wine
- 1/3 cup parmesan cheese, grated
- 1 teaspoon seasoned salt
- 1/3 teaspoon mixed peppercorns
- 1/2 teaspoon fennel seed

DIRECTIONS:

Add the parmesan cheese, salt, peppercorns, fennel seeds, and tarragon to your food processor; blitz for about 20 seconds.
Drizzle fish fillets with dry white wine. Dump the egg into a shallow dish.
Now, coat the fish fillets with the beaten egg on all sides; then, coat them with the seasoned cracker mix.
Air-fry at 345 degrees f for about 17 minutes.

NUTRITION:

Calories 210, Total Fat 5g, Saturated Fat 1g, Cholesterol 42mg, Sodium 352mg, Carbohydrates 9g, Fiber 1g, Sugars 1g, Protein 30g

SMOKED AND CREAMED WHITE FISH

20 minutes	15 minutes	4

INGREDIENTS
1/2 tablespoon yogurt
1/3 cup spring garlic, finely chopped
Fresh chopped chives, for garnish
3 eggs, beaten
1/2 teaspoon dried dill weed
1 teaspoon dried rosemary
1/3 cup scallions, chopped
1/3 cup smoked white fish, chopped
1 ½ tablespoons crème fraîche
1 teaspoon kosher salt
1 teaspoon dried marjoram
1/3 teaspoon ground black pepper, or more to taste
Cooking spray

DIRECTIONS:

Firstly, spritz four oven safe ramekins with cooking spray. Then, divide smoked whitefish, spring garlic, and scallions among greased ramekins. Crack an egg into each ramekin; add the crème, yogurt and all seasonings.
Now, air-fry approximately 13 minutes at 355 degrees f. Taste for doneness and eat warm garnished with fresh chives.

NUTRITION:

Calories 99, Total Fat 6g, Saturated Fat 2g, Cholesterol 24mg, Sodium 530mg, Carbohydrates 0,5g, Fiber 0g, Sugars 0,4g, Protein 11g

PARMESAN AND PAPRIKA BAKED TILAPIA

20 minutes	15 minutes	6

INGREDIENTS
1 cup parmesan cheese, grated
1 teaspoon paprika
1 teaspoon dried dill weed
2 pounds tilapia fillets
1/3 cup mayonnaise
1/2 tablespoon lime juice
Salt and ground black pepper, to taste

DIRECTIONS:

Mix the mayonnaise, parmesan, paprika, salt, black pepper, and dill weed until everything is thoroughly combined.
Then, drizzle tilapia fillets with the lime juice.
Cover each fish fillet with parmesan/mayo mixture; roll them in parmesan/paprika mixture. Bake at 335 for about 10 minutes. Serve and eat warm.

NUTRITION:

Calories 209, Total Fat 9g, Saturated Fat 3g, Cholesterol 54mg, Sodium 278mg, Carbohydrates 1,3g, Fiber 6g, Sugars 0,5g, Protein 29g

TANGY COD FILLETS

20 minutes	15 minutes	2

INGREDIENTS

1 ½ tablespoons sesame oil
1/2 heaping teaspoon dried parsley flakes
1/3 teaspoon fresh lemon zest, finely grated
2 medium-sized cod fillets
1 teaspoon sea salt flakes
A pinch of salt and pepper
1/3 teaspoon ground black pepper, or more to savor
1/2 tablespoon fresh lemon juice

DIRECTIONS:

Set the air fryer to cook at 375 degrees f. Season each cod fillet with sea salt flakes, black pepper and dried parsley flakes. Now, drizzle them with sesame oil.
Place the seasoned cod fillets in a single layer at the bottom of the cooking basket; air-fry approximately 10 minutes.
While the fillets are cooking, prepare the sauce by mixing the other ingredients. Serve cod fillets on four individual plates garnished with the creamy citrus sauce.

NUTRITION:

Calories 220, Total Fat 6g, Saturated Fat 5g, Cholesterol 36mg, Sodium 620mg, Carbohydrates 25g, Fiber 2g, Sugars 7g,Protein 16g

FISH AND CAULIFLOWER CAKES

140 minutes	13 minutes	4

INGREDIENTS

1/2 pound cauliflower florets
1/2 teaspoon english mustard
2 tablespoons butter, room temperature
1/2 tablespoon cilantro, minced
2 tablespoons sour cream
2 ½ cups cooked white fish
Salt and freshly cracked black pepper, to savor

DIRECTIONS:

Boil the cauliflower until tender. Then, purée the cauliflower in your blender. Transfer to a mixing dish.
Now, stir in the fish, cilantro, salt, and black pepper.
Add the sour cream, english mustard, and butter; mix until everything's well incorporated. Using your hands, shape into patties.
Place in the refrigerator for about 2 hours. Cook for 13 minutes at 395 degrees f. Serve with some extra english mustard.

NUTRITION:

Calories 280, Total Fat 12g, Saturated Fat 4g, Cholesterol 52mg, Sodium 272mg, Carbohydrates 21g, Fiber 2g, Sugars 0,5g, Protein 23g

MARINATED SCALLOPS WITH BUTTER AND BEER

70 minutes	7 minutes	4

INGREDIENTS

2 pounds sea scallops
1/2 cup beer
4 tablespoons butter
2 sprigs rosemary, only leaves
Sea salt and freshly cracked black pepper, to taste

DIRECTIONS:

In a ceramic dish, mix the sea scallops with beer; let it marinate for 1 hour.
Meanwhile, preheat your air fryer to 400 degrees f. Melt the butter and add the rosemary leaves. Stir for a few minutes.
Discard the marinade and transfer the sea scallops to the air fryer basket. Season with salt and black pepper.
Cook the scallops in the preheated air fryer for 7 minutes, shaking the basket halfway through the cooking time. Work in batches.

NUTRITION:

Calories 609, Total Fat 19g, Saturated Fat 4g, Cholesterol 214mg, Sodium 480mg, Carbohydrates 0,5g, Fiber 0g, Sugars 0,4g, Protein 28g

CHEESY FISH GRATIN

30 minutes	20 minutes	4

NGREDIENTS

tablespoon avocado oil
pound hake fillets
teaspoon garlic powder
ea salt and ground white pepper, to aste
tablespoons shallots, chopped
bell pepper, seeded and chopped
/2 cup cottage cheese
/2 cup sour cream
1 egg, well whisked
1 teaspoon yellow mustard
1 tablespoon lime juice
1/2 cup swiss cheese, shredded

DIRECTIONS:

Brush the bottom and sides of a casserole dish with avocado oil. Add the hake fillets to the casserole dish and sprinkle with garlic powder, salt, and pepper.
Add the chopped shallots and bell peppers.
In a mixing bowl, thoroughly combine the cottage cheese, sour cream, egg, mustard, and lime juice. Pour the mixture over fish and spread evenly.
Cook in the preheated air fryer at 370 degrees f for 10 minutes.
Top with the swiss cheese and cook an additional 7 minutes. Let it rest for 10 minutes before slicing and serving.

NUTRITION:

Calories 262, Total Fat 15g, Saturated Fat 6g, Cholesterol 64mg, Sodium 528mg, Carbohydrates 6g, Fiber 0g, Sugars 0g, Protein 23g

FIJAN COCONUT FISH

20 minutes +marinating time	15 minutes	2

Ingredients

1 cup coconut milk
2 tablespoons lime juice
2 tablespoons shoyu sauce
Salt and white pepper, to taste
1 teaspoon turmeric powder
1/2 teaspoon ginger powder
1/2 thai bird's eye chili, seeded and finely chopped
1 pound tilapia
2 tablespoons olive oil

Directions:

In a mixing bowl, thoroughly combine the coconut milk with the lime juice, shoyu sauce, salt, pepper, turmeric, ginger, and chili pepper. Add tilapia and let it marinate for 1 hour.
Brush the air fryer basket with olive oil. Discard the marinade and place the tilapia fillets in the air fryer basket.
Cook the tilapia in the preheated air fryer at 400 degrees f for 6 minutes; turn them over and cook for 6 minutes more. Work in batches.
Serve with some extra lime wedges if desired.

Nutrition:

Calories 240, Total Fat 15g, Saturated Fat 6g, Cholesterol 76mg, Sodium 720mg, Carbohydrates 13g, Fiber 3g, Sugars 5g,Protein 30g

SOLE FISH AND CAULIFLOWER FRITTERS

30 minutes	25 minutes	2

Ingredients

1/2 pound sole fillets
1/2 pound mashed cauliflower
1 egg, well beaten
1/2 cup red onion, chopped
2 garlic cloves, minced
2 tablespoons fresh parsley, chopped
1 bell pepper, finely chopped
1/2 teaspoon scotch bonnet pepper, minced
1 tablespoon olive oil
1 tablespoon coconut aminos
1/2 teaspoon paprika
Salt and white pepper, to taste

Directions:

Start by preheating your air fryer to 395 degrees f. Spritz the sides and bottom of the cooking basket with cooking spray.
Cook the sole fillets in the preheated air fryer for 10 minutes, flipping them halfway through the cooking time.
In a mixing bowl, mash the sole fillets into flakes. Stir in the remaining ingredients. Shape the fish mixture into patties.
Bake in the preheated air fryer at 390 degrees f for 14 minutes, flipping them halfway through the cooking time.

Nutrition:

Calories 60, Total Fat 4g, Saturated Fat 1g, Cholesterol 114mg, Sodium 82mg, Carbohydrates 3g, Fiber 1g, Sugars 1g, Protein 5g

FRENCH-STYLE SEA BASS

15 minutes	10 minutes	2

INGREDIENTS

1 tablespoon olive oil
2 sea bass fillets

<u>Sauce:</u>
1/2 cup mayonnaise
1 tablespoon capers, drained and chopped
1 tablespoon gherkins, drained and chopped
2 tablespoons scallions, finely chopped
2 tablespoons lemon juice

DIRECTIONS:

Start by preheating your air fryer to 395 degrees f. Drizzle olive oil all over the fish fillets.
Cook the sea bass in the preheated air fryer for 10 minutes, flipping them halfway through the cooking time.
Meanwhile, make the sauce by whisking the remaining ingredients until everything is well incorporated. Place in the refrigerator until ready to serve.

NUTRITION:

Calories 409, Total Fat 22g, Saturated Fat 7g, Cholesterol 234mg, Sodium 580mg, Carbohydrates 20g, Fiber 2g, Sugars 0,2g, Protein 22g

ASIAN-STYLE SALMON BURGERS

15 minutes	10 minutes	4

INGREDIENTS

1 pound salmon
1 egg
1 garlic clove, minced
2 green onions, minced
1 cup parmesan cheese
Sauce:
1 teaspoon rice wine
1 ½ tablespoons soy sauce
A pinch of salt
1 teaspoon gochugaru (korean red chili pepper flakes

DIRECTIONS:

Start by preheating your air fryer to 380 degrees f. Spritz the air fryer basket with cooking oil.
Mix the salmon, egg, garlic, green onions, and parmesan cheese in a bowl; knead with your hands until everything is well incorporated.
Shape the mixture into equally sized patties. Transfer your patties to the air fryer basket.
Cook the fish patties for 10 minutes, turning them over halfway through.
Meanwhile, make the sauce by whisking all ingredients. Serve the warm fish patties with the sauce on the side.

NUTRITION:

Calories 172, Total Fat 9g, Saturated Fat 2g, Cholesterol 101mg, Sodium 348mg, Carbohydrates 1g, Fiber 0g, Sugars 0g, Protein 21g

CRUSTED FLOUNDER FILLETS

20 minutes	12 minutes	2

INGREDIENTS

2 flounder fillets
1 egg
1/2 teaspoon worcestershire sauce
1/4 cup coconut flour
1/4 cup almond flour
1/2 teaspoon lemon pepper
1/2 teaspoon coarse sea salt
1/4 teaspoon chili powder

DIRECTIONS:

Rinse and pat dry the flounder fillets.
Whisk the egg and worcestershire sauce in a shallow bowl. In a separate bowl, mix the coconut flour, almond flour, lemon pepper, salt, and chili powder.
Then, dip the fillets into the egg mixture. Lastly, coat the fish fillets with the coconut flour mixture until they are coated on all sides.
Spritz with cooking spray and transfer to the air fryer basket. Cook at 390 degrees for 7 minutes.
Turn them over, spritz with cooking spray on the other side, and cook another 5 minutes.

NUTRITION:

Calories 190, Total Fat 5g, Saturated Fat 1g, Cholesterol 80mg, Sodium 299mg, Carbohydrates 5g, Fiber 0g, Sugars 0g,Protein 29g

PECAN CRUSTED TILAPIA

30 minutes	25 minutes	2

INGREDIENTS

2 tablespoons ground flaxseeds
1 teaspoon paprika
Sea salt and white pepper, to taste
1 teaspoon garlic paste
2 tablespoons extra-virgin olive oil
1/2 cup pecans, ground
5 tilapia fillets, slice into halves

DIRECTIONS:

Combine the ground flaxseeds, paprika, salt, white pepper, garlic paste, olive oil, and ground pecans in a ziploc bag. Add the fish fillets and shake to coat well.
Spritz the air fryer basket with cooking spray. Cook in the preheated air fryer at 400 degrees f for 10 minutes; turn them over and cook for 6 minutes more. Work in batches.
Serve with lemon wedges, if desired.

NUTRITION:

Calories 281, Total Fat 14g, Saturated Fat 2g, Cholesterol 2mg, Sodium 218mg, Carbohydrates 19g, Fiber 2g, Sugars 3g, Protein 19g

GRILLED SALMON WITH BUTTER AND WINE

45 minutes	10 minutes	4

INGREDIENTS

2 cloves garlic, minced
4 tablespoons butter, melted
Sea salt and ground black pepper, to taste
1 teaspoon smoked paprika
1/2 teaspoon onion powder
1 tablespoon lime juice
1/4 cup dry white wine
4 salmon steaks

DIRECTIONS:

Place all ingredients in a large ceramic dish. Cover and let it marinate for 30 minutes in the refrigerator.
Arrange the salmon steaks on the grill pan. Bake at 390 degrees for 5 minutes, or until the salmon steaks are easily flaked with a fork.
Flip the fish steaks, baste with the reserved marinade, and cook another 5 minutes.

NUTRITION:

Calories 391, Total Fat 21g, Saturated Fat 7g, Cholesterol 142mg, Sodium 120mg, Carbohydrates 5g, Fiber 1g, Sugars 0g, Protein 40g

GARLICKY GRILLED SHRIMP

35 minutes	5 minutes	4

NGREDIENTS

8 shrimps, shelled and deveined
tablespoons freshly squeezed lemon
ice
/2 teaspoon hot paprika
/2 teaspoon salt
teaspoon lemon-pepper seasoning
tablespoons extra-virgin olive oil
garlic cloves, peeled and minced
teaspoon onion powder
1/4 teaspoon cumin powder
1/2 cup fresh parsley, coarsely chopped

DIRECTIONS:

Place all the ingredients in a mixing dish; gently stir, cover and let it marinate for 30 minutes in the refrigerator.
Air-fry in the preheated air fryer at 400 degrees f for 5 minutes or until the shrimps turn pink.

NUTRITION:

Calories 187, Total Fat 9g, Saturated Fat 1g, Cholesterol 172mg, Sodium 170mg, Carbohydrates 2g, Fiber 0g, Sugars 0g, Protein 23g

TILAPIA WITH CHEESY CAPER SAUCE

15 minutes	12 minutes	4

Ingredients

4 tilapia fillets
1 tablespoon extra-virgin olive oil
Celery salt, to taste
Freshly cracked pink peppercorns, to taste
For the creamy caper sauce:
1/2 cup crème fraîche
2 tablespoons mayonnaise
1/4 cup cottage cheese, at room temperature
1 tablespoon capers, finely chopped

Directions:

Toss the tilapia fillets with olive oil, celery salt, and cracked peppercorns until they are well coated.
Place the fillets in a single layer at the bottom of the air fryer cooking basket. Air-fry at 360 degrees f for about 12 minutes; turn them over once during cooking.
Meanwhile, prepare the sauce by mixing the remaining items.
Lastly, garnish air-fried tilapia fillets with the sauce and serve immediately!

Nutrition:

Calories 271, Total Fat 22g, Saturated Fat 3g, Cholesterol 0mg, Sodium 371mg, Carbohydrates 2g, Fiber 0g, Sugars 0g,Protein 19g

JAPANESE FLOUNDER WITH CHIVES

15 minutes +marinating time	12 minutes	4

Ingredients

4 flounder fillets
Sea salt and freshly cracked mixed peppercorns, to taste
1 ½ tablespoons dark sesame oil
2 tablespoons sake
1/4 cup soy sauce
1 tablespoon grated lemon rind
2 garlic cloves, minced
2 tablespoons chopped chives, to serve

Directions:

Place all the ingredients, without the chives, in a large-sized mixing dish. Cover and allow it to marinate for about 2 hours in your fridge.
Remove the fish from the marinade and cook in the air fryer cooking basket at 360 degrees f for 10 to 12 minutes; flip once during cooking.
Pour the remaining marinade into a pan that is preheated over a medium-low heat; let it simmer, stirring continuously, until it has thickened.
Pour the prepared glaze over flounder and serve garnished with fresh chives.

Nutrition:

Calories 292, Total Fat 7g, Saturated Fat 1g, Cholesterol 115mg, Sodium 467mg, Carbohydrates 7g, Fiber 0g, Sugars 0g, Protein 42g

Poultry

PANKO CHICKEN BREAST

10 minutes | 15 minutes | 2

INGREDIENTS
1 large egg, beaten
1/4 cup flour, preferably all-purpose
3/4 cup panko bread crumbs
1/3 cup Parmesan, freshly grated
2 tsp lemon zest
1 tsp dried oregano
1/2 tsp cayenne pepper
Salt
Black pepper
2 chicken breasts, boneless skinless

DIRECTIONS:

Beat eggs in one bowl and spread the flour in another shallow bowl.
Whisk panko with cayenne, salt, black pepper, oregano, lemon zest, and parmesan in a shallow tray.
Take the chicken breasts and coat them with flour, then dip in eggs.
Coat the chicken breasts with the panko mixture and place them in the Air Fryer.
Place this Air Fryer inside the Ninja Foodi Oven and Close its lid.
Rotate the Ninja Foodi dial to select the "Air Fry" mode.
Press the Time button and again use the dial to set the cooking time to 10 minutes.
Now press the Temp button and rotate the dial to set the temperature at 350 degrees F.
Flip the chicken and return to cooking for another 5 minutes on the same mode and temperature.
Serve warm.

NUTRITION:

Calories 192, Total Fat 2g, Saturated Fat 0,5g, Cholesterol 65mg, Sodium 93mg, Carbohydrates 0,5g, Fiber 0g, Sugars 1g,Protein 29g

MAPLE CHICKEN THIGHS

10 minutes | 25 minutes | 4

INGREDIENTS
½ cup maple syrup
1 cup buttermilk
1 egg
1 tsp garlic powder
4 chicken thighs, skin-on, bone-in
Dry Rub:
½ cup flour, preferably all-purpose
½ tsp honey powder
1 tbsp of salt
1 tsp sweet paprika
¼ tsp smoked paprika
1 tsp onion powder
¼ tsp ground black pepper
¼ cup tapioca flour
½ tsp cayenne pepper
½ tsp garlic powder

DIRECTIONS:

Whisk buttermilk, egg, maple syrup, and a tsp of garlic in a Ziplock bag.
Add the chicken thighs to the buttermilk and seal this bag. Shake it to coat the chicken well then refrigerator for 1 hour.
Meanwhile, whisk the flour with salt, tapioca, pepper, smoked paprika, sweet paprika, honey powder, granulated garlic, cayenne pepper, and granulated onion in a bowl.
Remove the marinated chicken from its bag and coat it with the flour mixture.
Shake off the excess and place the chicken in the Air Fryer.
Place this sheet inside the Ninja Foodi oven and Close its lid.
Rotate the Ninja Foodi dial to select the "Air Fry" mode.
Press the Time button and again use the dial to set the cooking time to 12 minutes.
Now press the Temp button and rotate the dial to set the temperature at 380 degrees F.
Flip the chicken thighs and continue baking for another 13 minutes on the same temperature.
Serve warm.

NUTRITION:

Calories 282, Total Fat 6g, Saturated Fat 0g, Cholesterol 140mg, Sodium 580mg, Carbohydrates 20g, Fiber 0g, Sugars 18g, Protein 32g

ONE DISH CHICKEN BAKE

Prep time	Cook time	Servings
10 minutes	40 minutes	4

INGREDIENTS

1 can (14.5 oz.) canned tomatoes, diced
1 tbsp olive oil
2 tbsp fresh parsley, chopped
1 yellow onion, chopped
3 garlic cloves, minced
1 tsp dried oregano
4 boneless chicken breasts
Salt and black pepper, to taste
3/4 cup gruyere cheese, grated
1 tsp Italian seasoning
1 tbsp parsley, for garnish

DIRECTIONS:

Grease the Ninja baking dish with cooking spray.
Toss the tomatoes with olive oil, garlic, onions, Italian seasoning, oregano, and parsley in a bowl.
Spread this tomato mixture in the prepared baking dish.
Rub the chicken with salt, and black pepper then place over the tomatoes.
Transfer this baking dish to the Ninja oven and Close its lid.
Rotate the Ninja Foodi dial to select the "Bake" mode.
Press the Time button and again use the dial to set the cooking time to 35 minutes.
Now press the Temp button and rotate the dial to set the temperature at 400 degrees F.
Drizzle the cheese over the chicken and bake for 5 minutes.
Serve warm.

NUTRITION:

Calories 381, Total Fat 8g, Saturated Fat 2g, Cholesterol 138mg, Sodium 690mg, Carbohydrates 16g, Fiber 0g, Sugars 0g, Protein 47g

CRUMBED TENDERLOINS

Prep time	Cook time	Servings
10 minutes	12 minutes	4

NGREDIENTS

egg
½ cup dry bread crumbs
tbsp vegetable oil
chicken tenderloins

DIRECTIONS:

Whisk egg in a bowl and mix crumbs with oil in another bowl.
First, dip the chicken in the egg then coat well with crumbs mixture.
Shake off the excess then place the tenderloins in the Air Fryer.
Transfer this sheet to the Ninja Foodi Oven and Close its lid.
Rotate the Ninja Foodi dial to select the "Air Fry" mode.
Press the Time button and again use the dial to set the cooking time to 12 minutes.
Now press the Temp button and rotate the dial to set the temperature at 350 degrees F.
Serve warm.

NUTRITION:

Calories 257, Total Fat 11g, Saturated Fat 2g, Cholesterol 109mg, Sodium 170mg, Carbohydrates 10g, Fiber 0,5g, Sugars 1g, Protein 26g

10 minutes	12 minutes	2

INGREDIENTS

1 lb. chicken thighs, skinless, boneless
½ cup seasoned bread crumbs
1 tsp salt
½ tsp ground black pepper
¼ cup flour
1 egg, beaten
Avocado oil or cooking spray

CHICKEN SCHNITZEL

DIRECTIONS:

Place one chicken thigh in between 2 sheets of parchment sheet and use a mallet to flatten the chicken.
Similarly, flatten the remaining thighs using this method.
Now mix bread crumbs with black pepper and salt in a shallow bowl.
Spread flour in another bowl and whisk the egg in yet another bowl.
First coat the chicken with flour then dip into the egg.
Place the flatten chicken in the crumbs and flip to coat well, then shake off excess.
Keep the chicken thighs in the Air Fryer basket.
Transfer this Air Fryer to the Ninja Foodi oven and Close its lid.
Rotate the Ninja Foodi dial to select the "Air Fry" mode.
Press the Time button and again use the dial to set the cooking time to 6 minutes.
Now press the Temp button and rotate the dial to set the temperature at 375 degrees F.
Flip the cooked chicken and continue cooking for another 6 minutes on the same mode and temperature.
Serve warm.

NUTRITION:

Calories 412, Total Fat 13g, Saturated Fat 2g, Cholesterol 174mg, Sodium 383mg, Carbohydrates 35g, Fiber 2g, Sugars 2g,Protein 36g

10 minutes	15 minutes	4

INGREDIENTS

2 tbsp sesame oil
2 tbsp soy sauce
1 tbsp honey
1 tbsp sriracha sauce
1 tsp rice vinegar
2 lbs. chicken thighs
1 green onion, chopped
2 tbsp toasted sesame seeds

SESAME CHICKEN THIGHS

DIRECTIONS:

Whisk vinegar, sriracha, honey, soy sauce, and sesame oil in a large bowl.
Toss in chicken and mix well to coat it with sriracha sauce.
Cover this sriracha-honey chicken and refrigerate for 30 minutes to marinate.
Transfer the marinated chicken to the Air Fryer.
Place this Air Fryer to the Ninja Foodi Oven and Close its lid.
Rotate the Ninja Foodi dial to select the "Air Fry" mode.
Press the Time button and again use the dial to set the cooking time to 5 minutes.
Now press the Temp button and rotate the dial to set the temperature at 400 degrees F.
Flip the chicken and continue Air frying for another 10 minutes on the same mode and temperature.
Garnish with sesame seeds and green onions.
Serve warm.

NUTRITION:

Calories 283, Total Fat 13g, Saturated Fat 3g, Cholesterol 114mg, Sodium 1010mg, Carbohydrates 15g, Fiber 0g, Sugars 15g, Protein 30g

BAKED BUTTER THIGHS

10 minutes	35 minutes	6

INGREDIENTS

- Zest of 1 lemon
- 3 lb. (6) bone-in, skin-on chicken thighs
- Salt, to taste
- 1/2 cup butter
- 1 lb. baby potatoes, quartered
- 5 garlic cloves, minced
- 1 tbsp fresh thyme leaves
- 1 lemon, cut into rounds
- Black pepper, to taste
- 1 tbsp freshly chopped parsley, for garnish

DIRECTIONS:

Pat dry all the chicken thighs and rub them with salt and black pepper.
Whisk butter with lemon zest, thyme, and garlic in a small bowl.
Rub this butter thyme mixture over the chicken thighs liberally
Place these chicken thighs, potatoes, and lemon rounds in a casserole dish.
Transfer the casserole dish to the Ninja Foodi oven and Close its lid.
Rotate the Ninja Foodi dial to select the "Bake" mode.
Press the Time button and again use the dial to set the cooking time to 35 minutes.
Now press the Temp button and rotate the dial to set the temperature at 420 degrees F.
Serve warm.

NUTRITION:

Calories 213, Total Fat 12g, Saturated Fat 6g, Cholesterol 90mg, Sodium 170mg, Carbohydrates 8g, Fiber 0g, Sugars 0g, Protein 18g

PRIMAVERA CHICKEN

10 minutes	25 minutes	4

INGREDIENTS

- 4 boneless chicken breasts
- 2 tbsp olive oil
- Salt, to taste
- Black pepper, to taste
- 1 zucchini, sliced
- 3 medium tomatoes, sliced
- 1/2 red onion, sliced
- 1 cup mozzarella, cheese shredded
- 1 tsp Italian seasoning
- 2 yellow bell peppers, sliced
- Freshly parsley, for garnish

DIRECTIONS:

Carve one side slit in the chicken breasts and stuff them with all the veggies.
Place these stuffed chicken breasts in a casserole dish, then drizzle oil, Italian seasoning, black pepper, salt, and Mozzarella over the chicken.
Place this casserole dish in the Ninja Foodi Oven and Close its lid.
Rotate the Ninja Foodi dial to select the "Bake" mode.
Press the Time button and again use the dial to set the cooking time to 25 minutes.
Now press the Temp button and rotate the dial to set the temperature at 370 degrees F.
Garnish with parsley and serve warm.

NUTRITION:

Calories 343, Total Fat 5g, Saturated Fat 2g, Cholesterol 66mg, Sodium 970mg, Carbohydrates 40g, Fiber 7g, Sugars 1g, Protein 35g

Beef, Pork & Lamb

BAVARIAN BEEF SCHNITZEL

DIRECTIONS:

Season beef schnitzel with salt, cayenne pepper, and ground black pepper.

In a mixing dish, whisk the oil with coconut flour and parmesan cheese. In another bowl, whisk the eggs until pale and frothy.

Firstly, coat beef schnitzels with the whisked eggs; then, coat it with the parmesan mixture.

Air-fry for 10 minutes at 355 degrees f. Serve warm, garnished with lemon wedges and serve.

NUTRITION:

Calories 380, Total Fat 15g, Saturated Fat 8g, Cholesterol 99mg, Sodium 600mg, Carbohydrates 27g, Fiber 2g, Sugars 0g, Protein 32g

13 minutes	10 minutes	2

INGREDIENTS

2 medium-sized eggs
1 teaspoon cayenne pepper, or more to taste
1/4 cup coconut flour
1/4 cup parmesan cheese
1/3 freshly ground black pepper, or more to taste
Wedges of 1 fresh lemon, to serve

2 beef schnitzels
1 teaspoon fine sea salt
1 ½ tablespoons canola oil

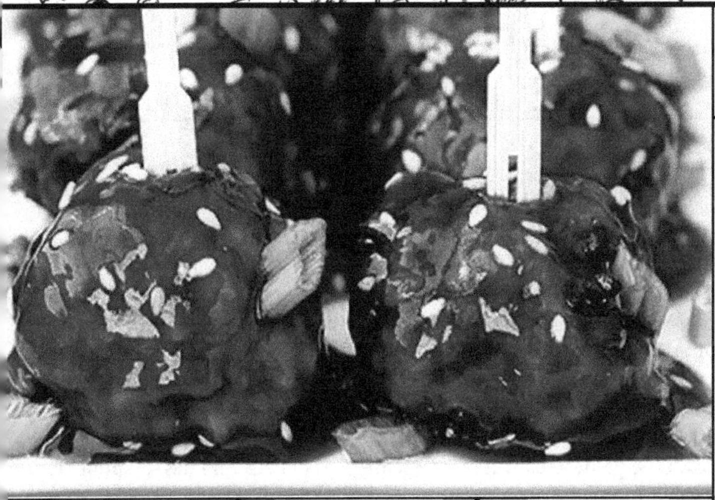

MEXICAN CHILI BEEF SAUSAGE MEATBALLS

DIRECTIONS:

Mix all ingredients in a bowl until the mixture has a uniform consistency.

Roll into bite-sized balls and transfer them to a baking dish.

Cook in the preheated air fryer at 345 degrees for 18 minutes. Serve on wooden sticks and enjoy!

NUTRITION:

Calories 243, Total Fat 16g, Saturated Fat 6g, Cholesterol 70mg, Sodium 470mg, Carbohydrates 10g, Fiber 1g, Sugars 3g, Protein 15g

25 minutes	18 minutes	4

INGREDIENTS

cup green onion, finely minced
/2 teaspoon parsley flakes
teaspoons onion flakes
pound chili sausage, crumbled
tablespoons flaxseed meal
cloves garlic, finely minced
teaspoon mexican oregano
tablespoon poblano pepper, hopped

Fine sea salt and ground black pepper, to taste
½ tablespoon fresh chopped sage

BBQ SKIRT STEAK

20 minutes + marinating time | 15 minutes | 5

INGREDIENTS

2 pounds skirt steak
2 tablespoons tomato paste
1 tablespoon olive oil
1 tablespoon coconut aminos
1/4 cup rice vinegar
1 tablespoon fish sauce
Sea salt, to taste
1/2 teaspoon dried dill
1/2 teaspoon dried rosemary
1/4 teaspoon black pepper, freshly cracked

DIRECTIONS:

Place all ingredients in a large ceramic dish; let it marinate for 3 hours in your refrigerator.
Coat the sides and bottom of the air fryer with cooking spray.
Add your steak to the cooking basket; reserve the marinade. Cook the skirt steak in the preheated air fryer at 400 degrees f for 12 minutes, turning over a couple of times, basting with the reserved marinade.

NUTRITION:

Calories 250, Total Fat 17g, Saturated Fat 5g, Cholesterol 54mg, Sodium 83mg, Carbohydrates 0g, Fiber 0g, Sugars 0g,Protein 22g

BEEF SAUSAGE AND VEGETABLE BOWL

35 minutes | 25 minutes | 4

INGREDIENTS

4 bell peppers
2 tablespoons canola oil
2 medium-sized tomatoes, halved
4 spring onions
4 beef sausages
1 tablespoon mustard

DIRECTIONS:

Start by preheating your air fryer to 400 degrees f.
Add the bell peppers to the cooking basket. Drizzle 1 tablespoon of canola oil all over the bell peppers.
Cook for 5 minutes. Turn the temperature down to 350 degrees f. Add the tomatoes and spring onions to the cooking basket and cook an additional 10 minutes.
Reserve your vegetables.
Then, add the sausages to the cooking basket. Drizzle with the remaining tablespoon of canola oil.
Cook in the preheated air fryer at 380 degrees f for 15 minutes, flipping them halfway through the cooking time.
Serve sausages with the air-fried vegetables and mustard; serve.

NUTRITION:

Calories 293, Total Fat 23g, Saturated Fat 8g, Cholesterol 54mg, Sodium 740mg, Carbohydrates 12g, Fiber 1g, Sugars 0,5g, Protein 12g

GRILLED MAYO SHORT LOIN STEAK

Directions:

Combine the mayonnaise, rosemary, worcestershire sauce, salt, pepper, paprika, and garlic; mix to combine well.
Now, brush the mayonnaise mixture over both sides of the steak. Lower the steak onto the grill pan.
Grill in the preheated air fryer at 390 degrees f for 8 minutes. Turn the steaks over and grill an additional 7 minutes.
Check for doneness with a meat thermometer. Serve warm.

20 minutes	15 minutes	4

Ingredients
- 1 cup mayonnaise
- 1 tablespoon fresh rosemary, finely chopped
- 2 tablespoons worcestershire sauce
- Sea salt, to taste
- 1/2 teaspoon ground black pepper
- 1 teaspoon smoked paprika
- 1 teaspoon garlic, minced
- 1 ½ pounds short loin steak

Nutrition:

Calories 513, Total Fat 22g, Saturated Fat 11g, Cholesterol 160mg, Sodium 700mg, Carbohydrates 18g, Fiber 0g, Sugars 5g, Protein 58g

BEEF FAJITA KETO BURRITO

Directions:

Toss the rump steak with the garlic powder, onion powder, cayenne pepper, piri piri powder, mexican oregano, salt, and black pepper.
Cook in the preheated air fryer at 390 degrees f for 10 minutes. Slice against the grain into thin strips. Add the cheese blend and cook for 2 minutes more.
Spoon the beef mixture onto romaine lettuce leaves; roll up burrito-style and serve.

20 minutes	12 minutes	4

Ingredients
- 1 pound rump steak
- 1 teaspoon garlic powder
- 1/2 teaspoon onion powder
- 1/2 teaspoon cayenne pepper
- 1 teaspoon piri piri powder
- 1 teaspoon mexican oregano
- Salt and ground black pepper, to taste
- 1 cup mexican cheese blend
- 1 head romaine lettuce, separated into leaves

Nutrition:

Calories 543, Total Fat 25g, Saturated Fat 8g, Cholesterol 126mg, Sodium 1070mg, Carbohydrates 20g, Fiber 7g, Sugars 7g, Protein 40g

WINE MARINATED FLANK STEAK

20 minutes
+ marinating time

12 minutes

4

Ingredients

1 ½ pounds flank steak
1/2 cup red wine
1/2 cup apple cider vinegar
2 tablespoons soy sauce
Salt, to taste
1/2 teaspoon ground black pepper
1/2 teaspoon red pepper flakes, crushed
1/2 teaspoon dried basil
1 teaspoon thyme

Directions:

Add all ingredients to a large ceramic bowl. Cover and let it marinate for 3 hours in your refrigerator.
Transfer the flank steak to the air fryer basket that is previously greased with nonstick cooking oil.
Cook in the preheated air fryer at 400 degrees f for 12 minutes, flipping over halfway through the cooking time.

Nutrition:

Calories 222, Total Fat 13g, Saturated Fat 4g, Cholesterol 56mg, Sodium 600mg, Carbohydrates 3g, Fiber 0g, Sugars 1g,Protein 23g

CLASSIC CUBE STEAK WITH SAUCE

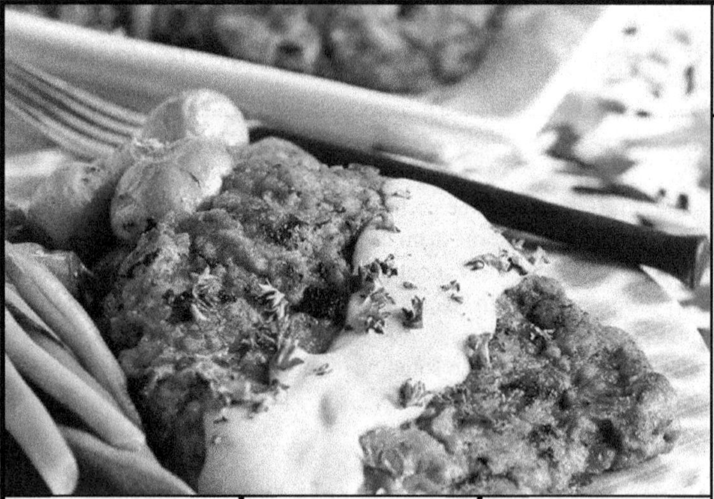

20 minutes

14 minutes

4

Ingredients

1 ½ pounds cube steak
Salt, to taste
1/4 teaspoon ground black pepper, or more to taste
4 ounces butter
2 garlic cloves, finely chopped
2 scallions, finely chopped
2 tablespoon fresh parsley, finely chopped
1 tablespoon fresh horseradish, grated
1 teaspoon cayenne pepper

Directions:

Pat dry the cube steak and season it with salt and black pepper. Spritz the air fryer basket with cooking oil. Add the meat to the basket.
Cook in the preheated air fryer at 400 degrees f for 14 minutes.
Meanwhile, melt the butter in a skillet over a moderate heat. Add the remaining ingredients and simmer until the sauce has thickened and reduced slightly.
Top the warm cube steaks with cowboy sauce and serve immediately.

Nutrition:

Calories 481, Total Fat 25g, Saturated Fat 14g, Cholesterol 128mg, Sodium 840mg, Carbohydrates 21g, Fiber 1g, Sugars 0,5g, Protein 41g

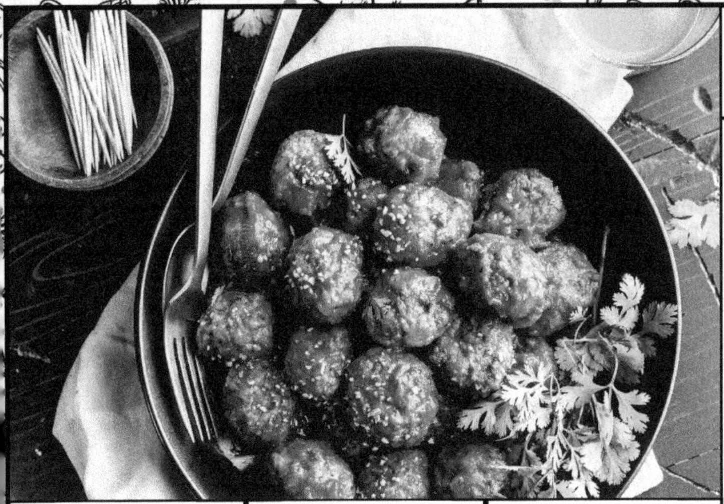

TANGY AND SAUCY BEEF FINGERS

DIRECTIONS:

Place the steak, red wine, lime juice, garlic powder, shallot powder, celery seeds, mustard seeds, salt, black pepper, and red pepper in a large ceramic bowl; let it marinate for 3 hours.

Tenderize the cube steak by pounding with a mallet; cut into 1-inch strips.

In a shallow bowl, whisk the eggs. In another bowl, mix the parmesan cheese and paprika.

Dip the beef pieces into the whisked eggs and coat on all sides. Now, dredge the beef pieces in the parmesan mixture.

Cook at 400 degrees f for 14 minutes, flipping halfway through the cooking time.

Meanwhile, make the sauce by heating the reserved marinade in a saucepan over medium heat; let it simmer until thoroughly warmed. Serve the steak fingers with the sauce on the side.

NUTRITION:

Calories 350, Total Fat 10g, Saturated Fat 1g, Cholesterol 70mg, Sodium 650mg, Carbohydrates 31g, Fiber 0g, Sugars 0g, Protein 30g

🕐 20 minutes + marinating time	🍽 14 minutes	🍴 4

INGREDIENTS
1 ½ pounds sirloin steak
1/4 cup red wine
1/4 cup fresh lime juice
1 teaspoon garlic powder
1 teaspoon shallot powder
1 teaspoon celery seeds
1 teaspoon mustard seeds
Coarse sea salt and ground black pepper, to taste
1 teaspoon red pepper flakes
2 eggs, lightly whisked
1 cup parmesan cheese
1 teaspoon paprika

SPICY T-BONE STEAK WITH AROMATICS

DIRECTIONS:

Rub the garlic halves all over the t-bone steak.

Drizzle the oil all over the steak and transfer it to the grill pan; grill the steak in the preheated air fryer at 400 degrees f for 10 minutes.

Meanwhile, whisk the tamari sauce, tomato paste, sriracha, vinegar, rosemary, and basil. Cook an additional 5 minutes

Serve garnished with fresh cilantro.

NUTRITION:

Calories 743, Total Fat 35g, Saturated Fat 15g, Cholesterol 256mg, Sodium 2670mg, Carbohydrates 2g, Fiber 1g, Sugars 0g, Protein 80g

🕐 20 minutes	🍽 15 minutes	🍴 3

INGREDIENTS
pound t-bone steak
garlic cloves, halved
tablespoons olive oil
1/4 cup tamari sauce
tablespoons tomato paste
teaspoon sriracha sauce
tablespoons white vinegar
teaspoon dried rosemary
1/2 teaspoon dried basil
2 heaping tablespoons cilantro, chopped

SAUCY LEMONY BEEF STEAKS

25 minutes | 18 minutes | 2

Ingredients

1 pound beef steaks
4 tablespoons white wine
2 teaspoons crushed coriander seeds
½ teaspoon fennel seeds
1/3 cup beef broth
2 tablespoons lemon zest, grated
2 tablespoons canola oil
1/2 lemon, cut into wedges
Salt flakes and freshly ground black pepper, to taste

Directions:

Heat the oil in a saucepan over a moderate flame. Then, cook the garlic for 1 minute, or until just fragrant.
Remove the pan from the heat; add the beef broth, wine, lemon zest, coriander seeds, fennel, salt flakes, and freshly ground black. Pour the mixture into a baking dish.
Add beef steaks to the baking dish; toss to coat well. Now, tuck the lemon wedges among the beef steaks.
Bake for 18 minutes at 335 degrees f. Serve warm.

Nutrition:

Calories 212, Total Fat 8g, Saturated Fat 2g, Cholesterol 64mg, Sodium 190mg, Carbohydrates 2g, Fiber 0g, Sugars 1g,Protein 26g

BEEF CHOPS WITH ENGLISH MUSTARD AND CORIANDER

35 minutes | 27 minutes | 3

Ingredients

1 ½ teaspoon english mustard
3 boneless beef chops
1/3 teaspoon garlic pepper
2 teaspoons oregano, dried
2 tablespoons vegetable oil
1 ½ tablespoons fresh coriander, chopped
1/2 teaspoon onion powder
1/2 teaspoon basil, dried
Grated rind of 1/2 small-sized lime
1/2 teaspoon fine sea salt

Directions:

Firstly, make the rub for the beef chops by mixing all the ingredients, except the chops and the new potatoes.
Now, evenly spread the beef chops with the english mustard rub.
Then, arrange the new potatoes in the bottom of the air fryer cooking basket. Top them with the prepared beef chops.
Roast for about 27 minutes at 365 degrees f, turning halfway through. Serve on individual plates with a keto salad on the side, if desired.

Nutrition:

Calories 187, Total Fat 18g, Saturated Fat 3g, Cholesterol 0mg, Sodium 1240mg, Carbohydrates 5g, Fiber 1g, Sugars 1g, Protein 38g

15 minutes	12 minutes	2

INGREDIENTS
1/2 cup vegetable stock
1/3 cup scallions, chopped
1 cloves garlic, minced
2 beef chops
½ tablespoon melted butter
Table salt and ground black pepper, to savor
For the salad:
1 ½ tablespoons freshly grated parmesan
1 tablespoon apple cider vinegar
2 tablespoons extra-virgin olive oil
2 cups very finely chopped or slivered curly kale
1/3 teaspoon ground black pepper, or more to taste
1 teaspoon table salt

BEEF WITH GREEN PARMESAN SALAD

DIRECTIONS:

Take an oven safe dish and toss beef chops with salt, pepper, butter, scallions, and garlic; pour in the stock; gently stir to coat.
Now, roast your chops at 395 degrees f for 12 to 14 minutes.
Meanwhile, make the parmesan-kale salad by mixing all salad components. Serve warm beef chops with the prepared kale salad.

NUTRITION:

Calories 350, Total Fat 16g, Saturated Fat 5g, Cholesterol 80mg, Sodium 490mg, Carbohydrates 13g, Fiber 3g, Sugars 1g, Protein 38g

20 minutes + marinating time	15 minutes	4

INGREDIENTS
1 ½ pounds short loin
2 tablespoons olive oil
2-3 cloves garlic, finely minced
1 cup leeks, sliced
1 bottle beer
1 rosemary sprig
2 thyme sprigs
1 teaspoon mustard seeds
1 bay leaf

BEER-BRAISED BEEF WITH LEEKS

DIRECTIONS:

Pat the beef dry; then, tenderize the beef with a meat mallet to soften the fibers. Place it in a large-sized mixing dish.
Add the remaining ingredients; toss to coat well and let it marinate for at least 1 hour.
Cook about 7 minutes at 395 degrees f; after that, pause the air fryer. Flip the meat over and cook for another 8 minutes, or until it's done.

NUTRITION:

Calories 353, Total Fat 15g, Saturated Fat 5g, Cholesterol 266mg, Sodium 750mg, Carbohydrates 10g, Fiber 2g, Sugars 4g, Protein 42g

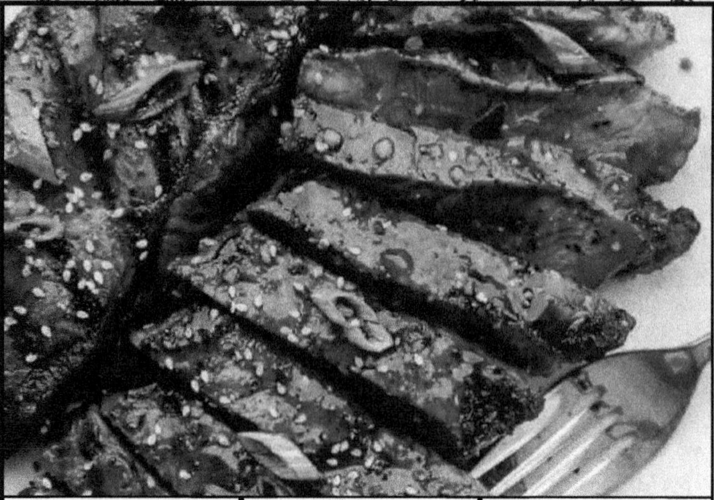

TERIYAKI STEAK WITH FRESH HERBS

40 minutes	28 minutes	4

Ingredients

2 heaping tablespoons fresh parsley, roughly chopped
1 pound beef rump steaks
2 heaping tablespoons fresh chives, roughly chopped
Salt and black pepper (or mixed peppercorns, to savor
For the sauce:
1/4 cup rice vinegar
1 tablespoon fresh ginger, grated
1 ½ tablespoons mirin
3 garlic cloves, minced
2 tablespoon rice bran oil
1/3 cup soy sauce
A few drops of liquid stevia

Directions:

Firstly, steam the beef rump steaks for 8 minutes (use the method of steaming that you prefer. Season the beef with salt and black pepper; scatter the chopped parsley and chives over the top.
Roast the beef rump steaks in an air fryer basket for 28 minutes at 345 degrees, turning halfway through.
While the beef is cooking, combine the ingredients for the teriyaki sauce in a sauté pan. Then, let it simmer over low heat until it has thickened.
Toss the beef with the teriyaki sauce until it is well covered and serve.

Nutrition:

Calories 322, Total Fat 18g, Saturated Fat 3g, Cholesterol 46mg, Sodium 2920mg, Carbohydrates 20g, Fiber 3g, Sugars 13g,Protein 24g

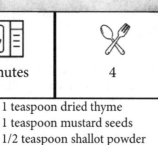

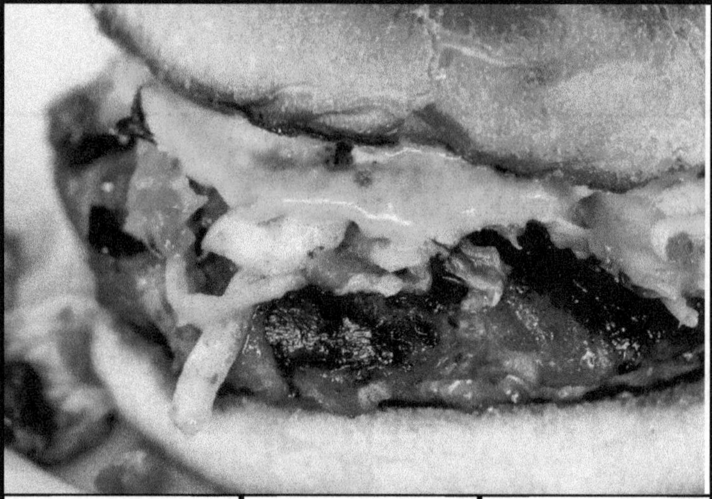

KOREAN BEEF BULGOGI BURGERS

20 minutes	18 minutes	4

Ingredients

1 ½ pounds ground beef
1 teaspoon garlic, minced
2 tablespoons scallions, chopped
Sea salt and cracked black pepper, to taste
1 teaspoon gochugaru (korean chili powder
1/2 teaspoon dried marjoram
1 teaspoon dried thyme
1 teaspoon mustard seeds
1/2 teaspoon shallot powder
1/2 teaspoon cumin powder
1/2 teaspoon paprika
1 tablespoon liquid smoke flavoring

Directions:

In a mixing bowl, thoroughly combine all ingredients until well combined. Shape into four patties and spritz them with cooking oil on both sides. Bake at 357 degrees f for 18 minutes, flipping over halfway through the cooking time. Serve warm.

Nutrition:

Calories 274, Total Fat 16g, Saturated Fat 6g, Cholesterol 74mg, Sodium 702mg, Carbohydrates 7g, Fiber 0,5g, Sugars 5g, Protein 22g

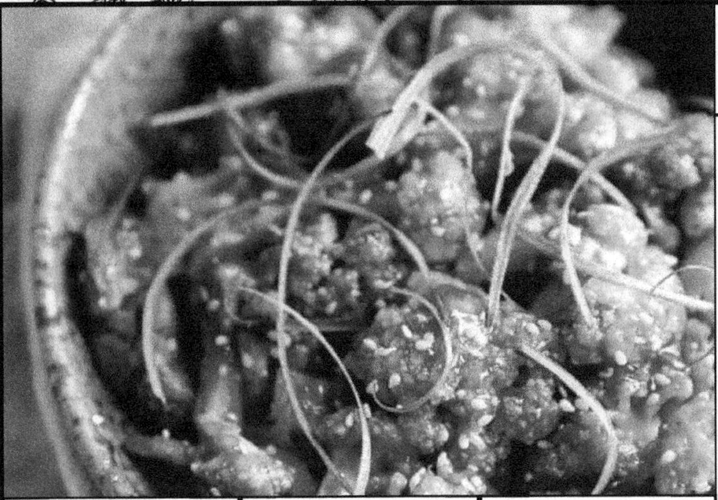

BEEF, PEARL ONIONS AND CAULIFLOWER

20 minutes + marinating time | 12 minutes | 4

INGREDIENTS

1 ½ pounds new york strip, cut into strips
1 (1-pound head cauliflower, broken into florets
1 cup pearl onion, sliced
Marinade:
1 tablespoon olive oil
2 cloves garlic, minced
1 teaspoon of ground ginger
1/4 cup tomato paste
1/2 cup red wine

DIRECTIONS:

Mix all ingredients for the marinade. Add the beef to the marinade and let it sit in your refrigerator for 1 hour.
Preheat your air fryer to 400 degrees f. Transfer the meat to the air fryer basket. Add the cauliflower and onions.
Drizzle a few tablespoons of marinade all over the meat and vegetables. Cook for 12 minutes, shaking the basket halfway through the cooking time. Serve warm.

NUTRITION:

Calories 410, Total Fat 20g, Saturated Fat 8g, Cholesterol 90mg, Sodium 380mg, Carbohydrates 6g, Fiber 1g, Sugars 4g, Protein 28g

ASIAN-STYLE ROUND STEAK

40 minutes + marinating time | 30 minutes | 4

NGREDIENTS

pounds top round steak, cut into ite-sized strips
garlic cloves, sliced
teaspoon dried marjoram
/4 cup red wine
tablespoon tamari sauce
alt and black pepper, to taste
tablespoon olive oil
red onion, sliced
2 bell peppers, sliced
1 celery stalk, sliced

DIRECTIONS:

Place the top round, garlic, marjoram, red wine, tamari sauce, salt and pepper in a bowl, cover and let it marinate for 1 hour.
Preheat your air fryer to 390 degrees f and add the oil.
Once hot, discard the marinade and cook the beef for 15 minutes.
Add the onion, peppers, carrot, and garlic and continue cooking until tender about 15 minutes more.
Open the air fryer every 5 minutes and baste the meat with the remaining marinade. Serve immediately.

NUTRITION:

Calories 333, Total Fat 7g, Saturated Fat 2g, Cholesterol 46mg, Sodium 777mg, Carbohydrates 42g, Fiber 8g, Sugars 3g, Protein 28g

Chicken and Turkey

RED THAI TURKEY DRUMSTICKS IN COCONUT MILK

25 minutes	23 minutes	2

INGREDIENTS
1 tablespoon red curry paste
1/2 teaspoon cayenne pepper
1 ½ tablespoons minced ginger
2 turkey drumsticks
1/4 cup coconut milk
1 teaspoon kosher salt, or more to taste
1/3 teaspoon ground pepper, to more to taste

DIRECTIONS:

First of all, place turkey drumsticks with all ingredients in your refrigerator; let it marinate overnight.
Cook turkey drumsticks at 380 degrees f for 23 minutes; make sure to flip them over at half-time. Serve with the salad on the side.

NUTRITION:

Calories 200, Total Fat 12g, Saturated Fat 6g, Cholesterol 75mg, Sodium 280mg, Carbohydrates 2g, Fiber 0,5g, Sugars 0,5g, Protein 21g

FRIED TURKEY WITH LEMON AND HERBS

45 minutes	28 minutes	6

INGREDIENTS
1 ½ tablespoons yellow mustard
1 ½ tablespoons herb seasoning blend
1/3 cup tamari sauce
1 ½ tablespoons olive oil
1/2 lemon, juiced
3 turkey drumsticks
1/3 cup pear or apple cider vinegar
2 sprigs rosemary, chopped

DIRECTIONS:

Dump all ingredients into a mixing dish. Let it marinate overnight.
Set your air fryer to cook at 355 degrees f.
Season turkey drumsticks with salt and black pepper and roast them at 355 degrees f for 28 minutes. Cook one drumstick at a time.
Pause the machine after 14 minutes and flip turkey drumstick.

NUTRITION:

Calories 722, Total Fat 37g, Saturated Fat 10g, Cholesterol 264mg, Sodium 777mg, Carbohydrates 3g, Fiber 1g, Sugars 0g, Protein 91g

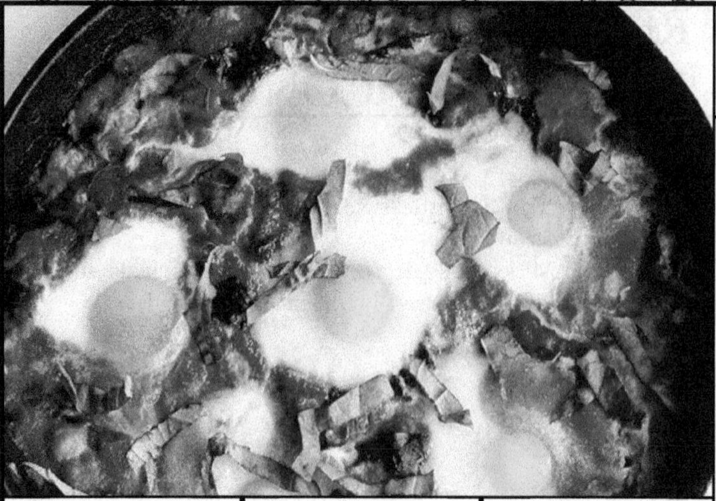

CHICKEN SAUSAGE WITH NESTLED EGGS

20 minutes	17 minutes	6

Ingredients

6 eggs
2 bell peppers, seeded and sliced
1 teaspoon dried oregano
1 teaspoon hot paprika
1 teaspoon freshly cracked black pepper
6 chicken sausages
1 teaspoon sea salt
1 1/2 shallots, cut into wedges
1 teaspoon dried basil

Directions:

Take four ramekins and divide chicken sausages, shallot, and bell pepper among those ramekins. Cook at 315 degrees f for about 12 minutes. Now, crack an egg into each ramekin. Sprinkle the eggs with hot paprika, basil, oregano, salt, and cracked black pepper. Cook for 5 more minutes at 405 degrees f.

Nutrition:

Calories 243, Total Fat 15g, Saturated Fat 4g, Cholesterol 236mg, Sodium 670mg, Carbohydrates 13g, Fiber 3g, Sugars 2g,Protein 18g

PARMESAN CHICKEN NUGGETS

10 minutes	8 minutes	4

Ingredients

1 pound chicken breast, ground
1 teaspoon hot paprika
2 teaspoon sage, ground
1/3 teaspoon powdered ginger
1/2 teaspoon dried thyme
1/3 teaspoon ground black pepper, to taste
1 teaspoon kosher salt
2 tablespoons melted butter
3 eggs, beaten
1/2 cup parmesan cheese, grated

Directions:

In a mixing bowl, thoroughly combine ground chicken together with spices and an egg. After that, stir in the melted butter; mix to combine well.
Whisk the remaining eggs in a shallow bowl.
Form the mixture into chicken nugget shapes; now, coat them with the beaten eggs; then, dredge them in the grated parmesan cheese.
Cook in the preheated air fryer at 405 degrees f for 8 minutes.

Nutrition:

Calories 304, Total Fat 8g, Saturated Fat 2g, Cholesterol 114mg, Sodium 395mg, Carbohydrates 9g, Fiber 0g, Sugars 1g, Protein 27g

TANGY AND BUTTERY CHICKEN

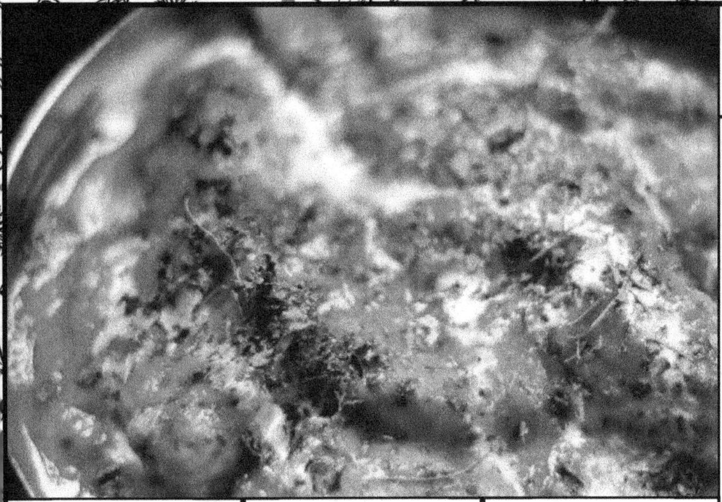

20 minutes	13 minutes	4

Ingredients

½ tablespoon worcestershire sauce
1 teaspoon finely grated orange zest
2 tablespoons melted butter
½ teaspoon smoked paprika
4 chicken drumsticks, rinsed and halved
1 teaspoon sea salt flakes
1 tablespoon cider vinegar
1/2 teaspoon mixed peppercorns, freshly cracked

Directions:

Firstly, pat the chicken drumsticks dry. Coat them with the melted butter on all sides. Toss the chicken drumsticks with the other ingredients. Transfer them to the air fryer cooking basket and roast for about 13 minutes at 345 degrees f.

Nutrition:

Calories 490, Total Fat 34g, Saturated Fat 14g, Cholesterol 180mg, Sodium 256mg, Carbohydrates 6g, Fiber 0,3g, Sugars 0,3g, Protein 41g

EASY TURKEY KABOBS

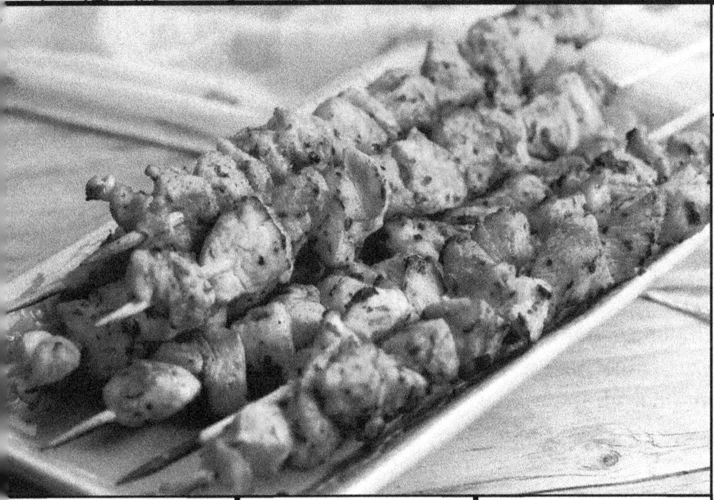

15 minutes	10 minutes	8

ngredients

cup parmesan cheese, grated
½ cups of water
4 ounces ground turkey
small eggs, beaten
teaspoon ground ginger
½ tablespoons vegetable oil
cup chopped fresh parsley
tablespoons almond meal
/4 teaspoon salt
1 heaping teaspoon fresh rosemary, finely chopped
1/2 teaspoon ground allspice

Directions:

Mix all of the above ingredients in a bowl. Knead the mixture with your hands.
Then, take small portions and gently roll them into balls.
Now, preheat your air fryer to 380 degrees f. Air fry for 8 to 10 minutes in the air fryer basket. Serve on a serving platter with skewers and eat with your favorite dipping sauce.

Nutrition:

Calories 243, Total Fat 15g, Saturated Fat 2g, Cholesterol 46mg, Sodium 807mg, Carbohydrates 10g, Fiber 2g, Sugars 1g, Protein 20g

TURKEY BREASTS WITH GREEK MUSTARD SAUCE

73 minutes	18 minutes	4

INGREDIENTS
1/2 teaspoon cumin powder
2 pounds turkey breasts, quartered
2 cloves garlic, smashed
½ teaspoon hot paprika
2 tablespoons melted butter
1 teaspoon fine sea salt
Freshly cracked mixed peppercorns, to savor
Fresh juice of 1 lemon
For the mustard sauce:
1 ½ tablespoons mayonnaise
1 ½ cups greek yogurt
1/2 tablespoon yellow mustard

DIRECTIONS:

Grab a medium-sized mixing dish and combine together the garlic an melted butter; rub this mixture evenly over the surface of the turkey. Add the cumin powder, followed by paprika, salt, peppercorns, and lemon juice. Place in your refrigerator at least 55 minutes.
Set your air fryer to cook at 375 degrees f. Roast the turkey for 18 minutes, turning halfway through; roast in batches.
In the meantime, make the mustard sauce by mixing all ingredients fo the sauce. Serve warm roasted turkey with the mustard sauce.

NUTRITION:

Calories 317, Total Fat 6g, Saturated Fat 1g, Cholesterol 164mg, Sodium 405mg, Carbohydrates 2g, Fiber 0g, Sugars 1g,Protein 58g

COUNTRY-STYLE NUTTY TURKEY BREAST

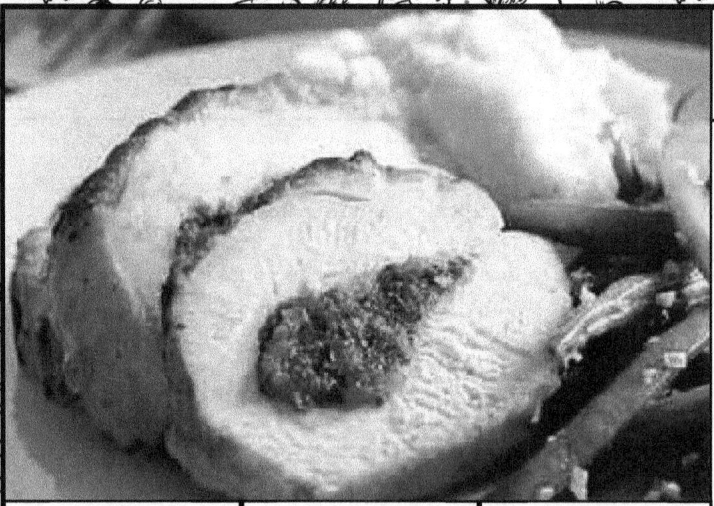

30 minutes	25 minutes	2

INGREDIENTS
1 ½ tablespoons coconut aminos
1/2 tablespoon xanthan gum
2 bay leaves
1/3 cup dry sherry
1 ½ tablespoons chopped walnuts
1 teaspoon shallot powder
1 pound turkey breasts, sliced
1 teaspoon garlic powder
2 teaspoons olive oil
1/2 teaspoon onion salt
1/2 teaspoon red pepper flakes, crushed
1 teaspoon ground black pepper

DIRECTIONS:

Begin by preheating your air fryer to 395 degrees f. Place all ingredients, minus chopped walnuts, in a mixing bowl and let them marinate at least 1 hour.
After that, cook the marinated turkey breast approximately 23 minutes or until heated through.
Pause the machine, scatter chopped walnuts over the top and air-fry a additional 5 minutes.

NUTRITION:

Calories 374, Total Fat 25g, Saturated Fat 8g, Cholesterol 142mg, Sodium 475mg, Carbohydrates 20g, Fiber 1g, Sugars 12g, Protein 40g

EGGS AND SAUSAGE WITH KETO ROLLS

40 minutes	14 minutes	6

INGREDIENTS

1 teaspoon dried dill weed
1 teaspoon mustard seeds
6 turkey sausages
3 bell peppers, seeded and thinly sliced
6 medium-sized eggs
1/2 teaspoon fennel seeds
1 teaspoon sea salt
1/3 teaspoon freshly cracked pink peppercorns

Keto rolls:

1/2 cup ricotta cheese, crumbled
1 cup part skim mozzarella cheese, shredded
1 egg
1/2 cup coconut flour
1/2 cup almond flour
1 teaspoon baking soda
2 tablespoons plain whey protein isolate

DIRECTIONS:

Set your air fryer to cook at 325 degrees f. Cook the sausages and bell peppers in the air fryer cooking basket for 8 minutes.
Crack the eggs into the ramekins; sprinkle them with salt, dill weed, mustard seeds, fennel seeds, and cracked peppercorns. Cook an additional 12 minutes at 395 degrees f.
To make the keto rolls, microwave the cheese for 1 minute 30 seconds, stirring twice. Add the cheese to the bowl of a food processor and blend well. Fold in the egg and mix again.
Add in the flour, baking soda, and plain whey protein isolate; blend again. Scrape the batter onto the center of a lightly greased cling film.
Form the dough into a disk and transfer to your freezer to cool; cut into 6 pieces and transfer to a parchment-lined baking pan (make sure to grease your hands.
Bake in the preheated oven at 400 degrees f for about 14 minutes.
Serve eggs and sausages on keto rolls.

NUTRITION:

Calories 300, Total Fat 24g, Saturated Fat 10g, Cholesterol 130mg, Sodium 526mg, Carbohydrates 1g, Fiber 0,5g, Sugars 1g, Protein 18g

BACON-WRAPPED TURKEY WITH CHEESE

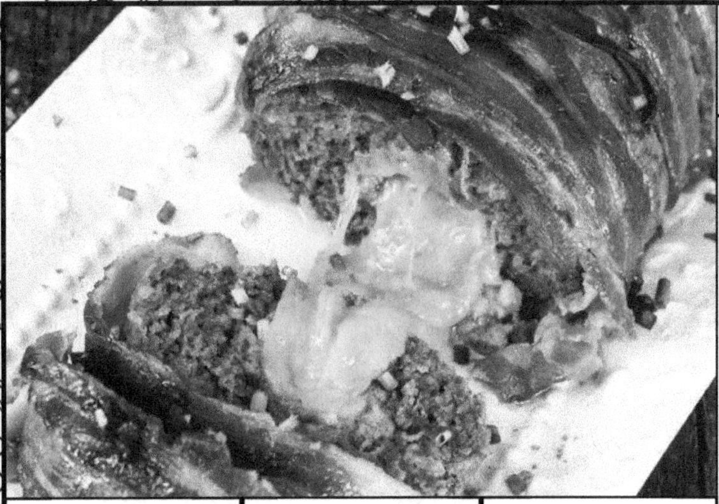

20 minutes	13 minutes	12

INGREDIENTS

1 ½ small-sized turkey breast, chop into 12 pieces
12 thin slices asiago cheese
Paprika, to taste
Fine sea salt and ground black pepper, to savor
12 rashers bacon

DIRECTIONS:

Lay out the bacon rashers; place 1 slice of asiago cheese on each bacon piece.
Top with turkey, season with paprika, salt, and pepper, and roll them up; secure with a cocktail stick.
Air-fry at 365 degrees f for 13 minutes.

NUTRITION:

Calories 342, Total Fat 15g, Saturated Fat 6g, Cholesterol 40mg, Sodium 966mg, Carbohydrates 34g, Fiber 8g, Sugars 6g, Protein 16g

ITALIAN-STYLE SPICY CHICKEN BREASTS

DIRECTIONS:

Sprinkle chicken breasts with the salt and sweet paprika; drizzle with chili sauce. Now, place a stick of asiago cheese in the middle of each chicken breast.

Then, tie the whole thing using a kitchen string; give a drizzle of sesame oil.

Transfer the stuffed chicken to the cooking basket. Add the other ingredients and toss to coat the chicken.

Afterward, cook for about 11 minutes at 395 degrees f. Serve the chicken on two serving plates, garnish with fresh or pickled salad and serve immediately.

20 minutes	11 minutes	4

INGREDIENTS

2 ounces asiago cheese, cut into sticks
1/3 cup tomato paste
1/2 teaspoon garlic paste
2 chicken breasts, cut in half lengthwise
1/2 cup green onions, chopped
1 tablespoon chili sauce
1/2 cup roasted vegetable stock
1 tablespoon sesame oil
1 teaspoon salt
2 teaspoons unsweetened cocoa
1/2 teaspoon sweet paprika, or more to taste

NUTRITION:

Calories 173, Total Fat 2,5g, Saturated Fat 0,5g, Cholesterol 68mg, Sodium 1792mg, Carbohydrates 10g, Fiber 3g, Sugars 2g,Protein 29g

CLASSIC CHICKEN NUGGETS

DIRECTIONS:

Start by preheating your air fryer to 390 degrees f.

Season each piece of the chicken with garlic salt, cayenne pepper, and black pepper.

In a mixing bowl, thoroughly combine the olive oil with protein powder and parmesan cheese. Dip each piece of chicken in the parmesan mixture.

Cook for 8 minutes, working in batches.

Later, if you want to warm the chicken nuggets, add them to the basket and cook for 1 minute more.

20 minutes	10 minutes	4

INGREDIENTS

1 ½ pounds chicken tenderloins, cut into small pieces
1/2 teaspoon garlic salt
1/2 teaspoon cayenne pepper
1/4 teaspoon black pepper, freshly cracked
4 tablespoons olive oil
2 scoops low-carb unflavored protein powder
4 tablespoons parmesan cheese, freshly grated

NUTRITION:

Calories 190, Total Fat 9g, Saturated Fat 1g, Cholesterol 10mg, Sodium 300mg, Carbohydrates 20g, Fiber 1g, Sugars 1g, Protein 8g

THAI CHICKEN WITH BACON

50 minutes | 20 minutes | 2

INGREDIENTS
4 rashers smoked bacon
2 chicken filets
1/2 teaspoon coarse sea salt
1/4 teaspoon black pepper, preferably freshly ground
1 teaspoon garlic, minced
1 (2-inch piece ginger, peeled and minced
1 teaspoon black mustard seeds
1 teaspoon mild curry powder
1/2 cup coconut milk
1/2 cup parmesan cheese, grated

DIRECTIONS:

Start by preheating your air fryer to 400 degrees f. Add the smoked bacon and cook in the preheated air fryer for 5 to 7 minutes. Reserve.
In a mixing bowl, place the chicken fillets, salt, black pepper, garlic, ginger, mustard seeds, curry powder, and milk. Let it marinate in your refrigerator about 30 minutes.
In another bowl, place the grated parmesan cheese.
Dredge the chicken fillets through the parmesan mixture and transfer them to the cooking basket. Reduce the temperature to 380 degrees f and cook the chicken for 6 minutes.
Turn them over and cook for a further 6 minutes. Repeat the process until you have run out of ingredients.
Serve with reserved bacon. Enjoy!

NUTRITION:

Calories 459, Total Fat 21g, Saturated Fat 8g, Cholesterol 178mg, Sodium 626mg, Carbohydrates 5g, Fiber 0,5g, Sugars 7g, Protein 23g

THANKSGIVING TURKEY WITH MUSTARD GRAVY

50 minutes | 45 minutes | 6

NGREDIENTS
: teaspoons butter, softened
teaspoon dried sage
sprigs rosemary, chopped
teaspoon salt
/4 teaspoon freshly ground black epper, or more to taste
whole turkey breast
tablespoons turkey broth
2 tablespoons whole-grain mustard
1 tablespoon butter

DIRECTIONS:

Start by preheating your air fryer to 360 degrees f.
To make the rub, combine 2 tablespoons of butter, sage, rosemary, salt, and pepper; mix well to combine and spread it evenly over the surface of the turkey breast.
Roast for 20 minutes in an air fryer cooking basket. Flip the turkey breast over and cook for a further 15 to 16 minutes. Now, flip it back over and roast for 12 minutes more.
While the turkey is roasting, whisk the other ingredients in a saucepan. After that, spread the gravy all over the turkey breast.
Let the turkey rest for a few minutes before carving.

NUTRITION:

Calories 190, Total Fat 15g, Saturated Fat 3g, Cholesterol 90mg, Sodium 234mg, Carbohydrates 2g, Fiber 3g, Sugars 2g, Protein 40g

LOADED TURKEY MEATLOAF WITH CHEESE

DIRECTIONS:

In a nonstick skillet, that is preheated over a moderate heat, sauté the turkey mince, scallions, garlic, thyme, and basil until just tender and fragrant.

Then set your air fryer to cook at 360 degrees. Combine sautéed mixture with the cheese and tamari sauce; then form the mixture into a loaf shape.

Mix the remaining items and pour them over the meatloaf. Cook in the air fryer baking pan for 45 to 47 minutes. Eat warm.

⏰ 50 minutes	🍲 45 minutes	🍴 6

INGREDIENTS

2 pounds turkey mince
1/2 cup scallions, finely chopped
2 garlic cloves, finely minced
1 teaspoon dried thyme
1/2 teaspoon dried basil
3/4 cup colby cheese, shredded
1 tablespoon tamari sauce
Salt and black pepper, to your liking
1/4 cup roasted red pepper tomato sauce
3/4 tablespoons olive oil
1 medium-sized egg, well beaten

NUTRITION:

Calories 243, Total Fat 12g, Saturated Fat 6g, Cholesterol 68mg, Sodium 792mg, Carbohydrates 11g, Fiber 0g, Sugars 5g, Protein 21g

CLASSIC CHICKEN NUGGETS

DIRECTIONS:

Take a baking dish that easily fits into your device; place the vegetables on the bottom of the baking dish and pour in roasted vegetable broth. In a large-sized mixing dish, place the remaining ingredients; let them marinate for about 30 minutes. Lay them on the top of the vegetables. Roast at 330 degrees f for 40 to 45 minutes.

⏰ 75 minutes	🍲 45 minutes	🍴 4

NUTRITION:

Calories 195, Total Fat 12g, Saturated Fat 4g, Cholesterol 10mg, Sodium 642mg, Carbohydrates 4g, Fiber 1g, Sugars 2g, Protein 19g

INGREDIENTS

1 red onion, cut into wedges
1 carrot, trimmed and sliced
1 celery stalk, trimmed and sliced
1 cup brussel sprouts, trimmed and halved
1 cup roasted vegetable broth
1 tablespoon apple cider vinegar
4 turkey thighs
1/2 teaspoon mixed peppercorns, freshly cracked
1 teaspoon fine sea salt
1 teaspoon cayenne pepper
1 teaspoon onion powder
1/2 teaspoon garlic powder
1/3 teaspoon mustard seeds

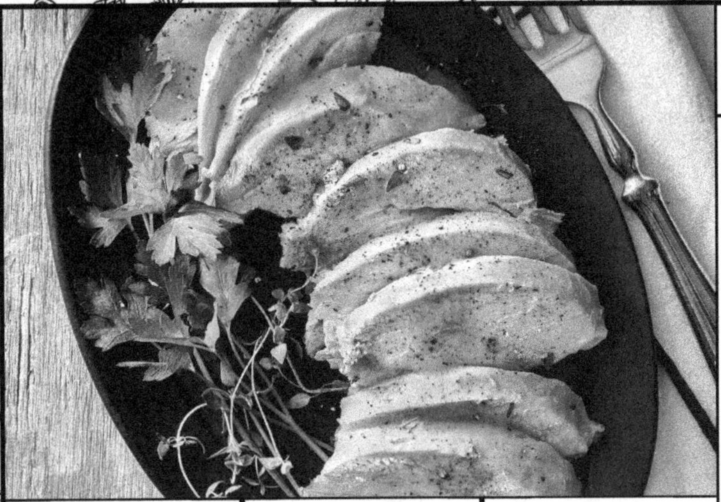

AROMATIC TURKEY BREAST WITH MUSTARD

DIRECTIONS:

Set your air fryer to cook at 365 degrees f.
Brush the turkey breast with olive oil and sprinkle with seasonings.
Cook at 365 degrees f for 45 minutes, turning twice. Now, pause the machine and spread the cooked breast with the hot mustard.
Air-fry for 6 to 8 more minutes. Let it rest before slicing and serving.

NUTRITION:

Calories 148, Total Fat 1g, Saturated Fat 0g, Cholesterol 78mg, Sodium 426mg, Carbohydrates 1g, Fiber 0,5g, Sugars 0g, Protein 30g

 60 minutes | 45 minutes | 4

INGREDIENTS

1/2 teaspoon dried thyme
1 ½ pounds turkey breasts
1/2 teaspoon dried sage
3 whole star anise
1 ½ tablespoons olive oil
1 ½ tablespoons hot mustard
1 teaspoon smoked cayenne pepper
1 teaspoon fine sea salt

RUSTIC TURKEY BREASTS

DIRECTIONS:

Combine sage leaves, lemon juice, mustard, garlic, and paprika in a small-sized mixing bowl; mix thoroughly until everything is well combined.
Then, smear this mixture on the turkey breast. Add white wine and let it marinate about 2 hours.
Transfer to the air fryer cooking basket along with the leeks. Drizzle olive oil over everything.
Bake at 375 degrees f for 48 minutes, turning once or twice.

NUTRITION:

Calories 120, Total Fat 1g, Saturated Fat 0g, Cholesterol 70mg, Sodium 54mg, Carbohydrates 0g, Fiber 0g, Sugars 0g, Protein 28g

50 minutes + marinating time | 45 minutes | 4

INGREDIENTS

1 ½ pounds turkey breasts, boneless and skinless
1/2 palmful chopped fresh sage leaves
1 ½ tablespoons freshly squeezed lemon juice
1/3 teaspoon dry mustard
1/3 cup dry white wine
3 cloves garlic, minced
2 leeks, cut into thick slices
1/2 teaspoon smoked paprika
2 tablespoons olive oil

Dessert

PERFECT MINI CHEESECAKES

40 minutes	35 minutes	6

INGREDIENTS

1/2 cup almond flour
1 ½ tablespoons unsalted butter, melted
2 tablespoons erythritol
1 (8-ounce package cream cheese, softened
1/4 cup powdered erythritol
1/2 teaspoon vanilla paste
1 egg, at room temperature

Topping:

1 ½ cups sour cream
3 tablespoons powdered erythritol
1 teaspoon vanilla extract

DIRECTIONS:

Thoroughly combine the almond flour, butter, and 2 tablespoons of erythritol in a mixing bowl. Press the mixture into the bottom of lightly greased custard cups.
Then, mix the cream cheese, 1/4 cup of powdered erythritol, vanilla, and egg using an electric mixer on low speed. Pour the batter into the pan, covering the crust.
Bake in the preheated air fryer at 330 degrees f for 35 minutes until edges are puffed and the surface is firm.
Mix the sour cream, 3 tablespoons of powdered erythritol, and vanilla for the topping; spread over the crust and allow it to cool to room temperature.
Transfer to your refrigerator for 6 to 8 hours. Serve well chilled.

NUTRITION:

Calories 119, Total Fat 4g, Saturated Fat 2g, Cholesterol 37mg, Sodium 216mg, Carbohydrates 14g, Fiber 0g, Sugars 10g, Protein 6g

CLASSIC COOKIES WITH HAZELNUTS

20 minutes	10 minutes	6

NGREDIENTS

. cup almond flour
/2 cup coconut flour
teaspoon baking soda
. teaspoon fine sea salt
stick butter
cup swerve
teaspoons vanilla
eggs, at room temperature
1 cup hazelnuts, coarsely chopped

DIRECTIONS:

Begin by preheating your air fryer to 350 degrees f.
Mix the flour with the baking soda, and sea salt.
In the bowl of an electric mixer, beat the butter, swerve, and vanilla until creamy. Fold in the eggs, one at a time, and mix until well combined.
Slowly and gradually, stir in the flour mixture. Finally, fold in the coarsely chopped hazelnuts.
Divide the dough into small balls using a large cookie scoop; drop onto the prepared cookie sheets. Bake for 10 minutes or until golden brown, rotating the pan once or twice through the cooking time.
Work in batches and cool for a couple of minutes before removing to wire racks and serve.

NUTRITION:

Calories 110, Total Fat 6g, Saturated Fat 2g, Cholesterol 11mg, Sodium 64mg, Carbohydrates 12g, Fiber 0g, Sugars 8g, Protein 1g

CHOCOLATE ALMOND COOKIES

20 minutes	15 minutes	10

Ingredients

- 2 cups almond flour
- 1/2 cup coconut flour
- 5 ounces swerve
- 5 ounces butter, softened
- 1 egg, beaten
- 1 teaspoon vanilla essence
- 4 ounces double cream
- 3 ounces bakers' chocolate, unsweetened
- 1 teaspoon cardamom seeds, finely crushed

Directions:

Start by preheating your air fryer to 350 degrees f.
In a mixing bowl, thoroughly combine the flour, swerve, and butter. Mix until your mixture resembles breadcrumbs.
Gradually, add the egg and vanilla essence. Shape your dough into small balls and place in the parchment-lined air fryer basket.
Bake in the preheated air fryer for 10 minutes. Rotate the pan and bake for another 5 minutes. Transfer the freshly baked cookies to a cooling rack.
As the biscuits are cooling, melt the double cream and bakers' chocolate in the air fryer safe bowl at 350 degrees f. Add the cardamom seeds and stir well.
Spread the filling over the cooled biscuits and sandwich together and serve.

Nutrition:

Calories 225, Total Fat 17g, Saturated Fat 4g, Cholesterol 20mg, Sodium 62mg, Carbohydrates 17g, Fiber 2g, Sugars 12g,Protein 4g

CHOCOLATE FUDGY BROWNIES

30 minutes	20 minutes	8

Ingredients

- 1 stick butter, melted
- 1 cup swerve
- 2 eggs
- 1 teaspoon vanilla essence
- 2 tablespoons flaxseed meal
- 1 cup coconut flour
- 1 teaspoon baking powder
- 1/2 cup cocoa powder, unsweetened
- A pinch of salt
- A pinch of ground cardamom

Directions:

Start by preheating your air fryer to 350 degrees f. Now, spritz the sides and bottom of a baking pan with cooking spray.
In a mixing dish, beat the melted butter with swerve until fluffy. Next, fold in the eggs and beat again.
After that, add the vanilla, flour, baking powder, cocoa, salt, and ground cardamom. Mix until everything is well combined.
Bake in the preheated air fryer for 20 to 22 minutes. Enjoy!

Nutrition:

Calories 126, Total Fat 5g, Saturated Fat 2g, Cholesterol 37mg, Sodium 81mg, Carbohydrates 20g, Fiber 1g, Sugars 12g, Protein 2g

FLUFFY CHOCOLATE AND COCONUT CAKE

DIRECTIONS:

Begin by preheating your air fryer to 330 degrees f.
In a microwave-safe bowl, melt the butter, chocolate, and stevia.
Add the other ingredients to the cooled chocolate mixture; stir to combine well. Scrape the batter into a lightly greased baking pan.
Bake in the preheated air fryer for 15 minutes or until the center is springy and a toothpick comes out dry. Enjoy!

NUTRITION:

Calories 194, Total Fat 11g, Saturated Fat 8g, Cholesterol 98mg, Sodium 42mg, Carbohydrates 20g, Fiber 1g, Sugars 17g, Protein 6g

20 minutes	15 minutes	6

INGREDIENTS
1/2 stick butter, at room temperature
1/2 cup chocolate, unsweetened and chopped
1 tablespoon liquid stevia
1 ½ cups coconut flour
A pinch of fine sea salt
2 eggs, whisked

1/2 teaspoon vanilla extract

ESPRESSO BROWNIES WITH MASCARPONE FROSTING

For the chocolate mascarpone frosting:	1 ½ cups confectioner's swerve
4 ounces mascarpone cheese, at room temperature	1/4 cup unsalted butter, at room temperature
	1 teaspoon vanilla paste
1 ½ ounces unsweetened chocolate chips	A pinch of fine sea salt

DIRECTIONS:

First of all, microwave the chocolate and almond butter until completely melted; allow the mixture to cool at room temperature.
Then, whisk the eggs, swerve, cinnamon, espresso powder, coffee extract, ancho chile powder, and lime zest.
Next step, add the vanilla/egg mixture to the chocolate/butter mixture.
Stir in the almond meal and coconut flour along with baking soda, baking powder and cocoa powder.
Finally, press the batter into a lightly buttered cake pan. Air-fry for 35 minutes at 345 degrees f.
In the meantime, make the frosting. Beat the butter and mascarpone cheese until creamy. Add in the melted chocolate chips and vanilla paste.
Gradually, stir in the confectioner's swerve and salt; beat until everything's well combined. Lastly, frost the brownies and serve.

NUTRITION:
Calories 360, Total Fat 33g, Saturated Fat 9g, Cholesterol 110mg, Sodium 44mg, Carbohydrates 10g, Fiber 0g, Sugars 8g, Protein 6g

40 minutes	35 minutes	8

INGREDIENTS
5 ounces unsweetened chocolate, chopped into chunks
2 tablespoons instant espresso powder
1 tablespoon cocoa powder, unsweetened
1/2 cup almond butter
1/2 cup almond meal

3/4 cup swerve
1 teaspoon pure coffee extract
1/2 teaspoon lime peel zest
1/4 cup coconut flour
2 eggs plus 1 egg yolk
1/2 teaspoon baking soda
1/2 teaspoon baking powder
1/2 teaspoon ground cinnamon
1/3 teaspoon ancho chile powder

COCONUT AND ORANGE CAKE

30 minutes	17 minutes	6

INGREDIENTS

3/4 cup coconut flour
1/3 cup coconut milk
2 tablespoons orange jam, unsweetened
1 stick butter
3/4 cup granulated swerve
2 eggs
1 ¼ cups almond flour
1/2 teaspoon baking powder
1/3 teaspoon grated nutmeg
1/4 teaspoon salt

DIRECTIONS:

Set the air fryer to cook at 355 degrees f. Spritz the inside of a cake pan with the cooking spray. Then, beat the butter with granulated swerve until fluffy.
Fold in the eggs; continue mixing until smooth. Throw in the coconut flour, salt, and nutmeg; then, slowly and carefully pour in the coconut milk.
Finally, add almond flour, baking powder and orange jam; mix thoroughly to create the cake batter.
Then, press the batter into the cake pan. Bake for 17 minutes and transfer your cake to a cooling rack. Frost the cake and serve chilled. Enjoy!

NUTRITION:

Calories 290, Total Fat 17g, Saturated Fat 4g, Cholesterol 60mg, Sodium 362mg, Carbohydrates 33g, Fiber 1g, Sugars 12g,Protein 4g

OLD-FASHIONED WALNUT AND RUM COOKIES

40 minutes	35 minutes	8

INGREDIENTS

1/2 cup walnuts, ground
1/2 cup coconut flour
1 cup almond flour
3/4 cup swerve
1 stick butter, room temperature
2 tablespoons rum
1/2 teaspoon pure vanilla extract
1/2 teaspoon pure almond extract

DIRECTIONS:

In a mixing dish, beat the butter with swerve, vanilla, and almond extract until light and fluffy. Then, throw in the flour and ground walnuts; add in rum.
Continue mixing until it forms a soft dough. Cover and place in the refrigerator for 20 minutes. In the meantime, preheat the air fryer to 330 degrees f.
Roll the dough into small cookies and place them on the air fryer cake pan; gently press each cookie using a spoon.
Bake butter cookies for 15 minutes in the preheated air fryer. Bon appétit!

NUTRITION:

Calories 226, Total Fat 20g, Saturated Fat 6g, Cholesterol 67mg, Sodium 121mg, Carbohydrates 5g, Fiber 1g, Sugars 3g, Protein 1g

CHOCOLATE AND BLUEBERRY CUPCAKES

20 minutes | 15 minutes | 6

INGREDIENTS
- 3 teaspoons cocoa powder, unsweetened
- 1/2 cup blueberries
- 1 ¼ cups almond flour
- 1/2 cup milk
- 1 stick butter, room temperature
- 3 eggs
- 3/4 cup granulated erythritol
- 1 teaspoon pure rum extract
- 1/2 teaspoon baking soda
- 1 teaspoon baking powder
- 1/4 teaspoon grated nutmeg
- 1/2 teaspoon ground cinnamon
- 1/8 teaspoon salt

DIRECTIONS:

Grab two mixing bowls. In the first bowl, thoroughly combine the erythritol, almond flour, baking soda, baking powder, salt, nutmeg, cinnamon and cocoa powder.
Take the second bowl and cream the butter, egg, rum extract, and milk; whisk to combine well. Now, add the wet mixture to the dry mixture. Fold in blueberries.
Press the prepared batter mixture into a lightly greased muffin tin. Bake at 345 degrees for 15 minutes. Use a toothpick to check if your cupcakes are baked. Bon appétit!

NUTRITION:

Calories 294, Total Fat 27g, Saturated Fat 8g, Cholesterol 108mg, Sodium 132mg, Carbohydrates 8g, Fiber 1g, Sugars 7g, Protein 4g

EASY FRUITCAKE WITH CRANBERRIES

40 minutes | 35 minutes | 8

NGREDIENTS
- cup almond flour
- /3 teaspoon baking soda
- /3 teaspoon baking powder
- /4 cup erythritol
- /2 teaspoon ground cloves
- /3 teaspoon ground cinnamon
- /2 teaspoon cardamom
- stick butter
- /2 teaspoon vanilla paste
- 2 eggs plus 1 egg yolk, beaten
- 1/2 cup cranberries, fresh or thawed
- 1 tablespoon browned butter

For ricotta frosting:
- 1/2 stick butter
- 1/2 cup firm ricotta cheese
- 1 cup powdered erythritol
- 1/4 teaspoon salt
- Zest of 1/2 lemon

DIRECTIONS:

Start by preheating your air fryer to 355 degrees f.
In a mixing bowl, combine the flour with baking soda, baking powder, erythritol, ground cloves, cinnamon, and cardamom.
In a separate bowl, whisk 1 stick butter with vanilla paste; mix in the eggs until light and fluffy. Add the flour/sugar mixture to the butter/egg mixture. Fold in the cranberries and browned butter.
Scrape the mixture into the greased cake pan. Then, bake in the preheated air fryer for about 20 minutes.
Meanwhile, in a food processor, whip 1/2 stick of the butter and ricotta cheese until there are no lumps.
Slowly add the powdered erythritol and salt until your mixture has reached a thick consistency. Stir in the lemon zest; mix to combine and chill completely before using.
Frost the cake and serve.

NUTRITION:

Calories 340, Total Fat 33g, Saturated Fat 9g, Cholesterol 80mg, Sodium 570mg, Carbohydrates 40g, Fiber 2g, Sugars 30g, Protein 4g

CLASSIC WHITE CHOCOLATE COOKIES

40 minutes	11 minutes	10

Ingredients

3/4 cup butter
1 2/3 cups almond flour
1/2 cup coconut flour
2 tablespoons coconut oil
3/4 cup granulated swerve
1/3 teaspoon ground anise star
1/3 teaspoon ground allspice
1/3 teaspoon grated nutmeg
1/4 teaspoon fine sea salt
8 ounces white chocolate, unsweetened
2 eggs, well beaten

Directions:

Put all of the above ingredients, minus 1 egg, into a mixing dish. Then, knead with hand until a soft dough is formed. Place in the refrigerator for 20 minutes.
Roll the chilled dough into small balls; flatten your balls and preheat the air fryer r to 350 degrees f.
Make an egg wash by using the remaining egg. Then, glaze the cookies with the egg wash; bake about 11 minutes and serve.

Nutrition:

Calories 290, Total Fat 15g, Saturated Fat 7g, Cholesterol 40mg, Sodium 162mg, Carbohydrates 39g, Fiber 1g, Sugars 25g,Protein 4g

FLUFFY COCONUT AND PECAN COOKIES

30 minutes	25 minutes	10

Ingredients

3/4 cup coconut oil, room temperature
1 ½ cups coconut flour
1 cup pecan nuts, unsalted and roughly chopped
3 eggs plus an egg yolk, whisked
1 ½ cups extra-fine almond flour
3/4 cup monk fruit
1/4 teaspoon freshly grated nutmeg
1/3 teaspoon ground cloves
1/2 teaspoon baking powder
1/3 teaspoon baking soda
1/2 teaspoon pure vanilla extract
1/2 teaspoon pure coconut extract
1/8 teaspoon fine sea salt

Directions:

In a bowl, combine both types of flour, baking soda and baking powder. In a separate bowl, beat the eggs with coconut oil. Combine egg mixture with the flour mixture.
Throw in the other ingredients, mixing well. Shape the mixture into cookies.
Bake at 370 degrees f for about 25 minutes and serve.

Nutrition:

Calories 146, Total Fat 9g, Saturated Fat 4g, Cholesterol 10mg, Sodium 135mg, Carbohydrates 10g, Fiber 1g, Sugars 9g, Protein 1g

FLOURLESS ALMOND AND GINGER COOKIES

50 minutes	45 minutes	8

INGREDIENTS
1/2 cup slivered almonds
1 stick butter, room temperature
4 ounces monk fruit
2/3 cup blanched almond flour
1/3 cup coconut flour
1/3 teaspoon ground cloves
1 tablespoon ginger powder
3/4 teaspoon pure vanilla extract

DIRECTIONS:

In a mixing dish, beat the monk fruit, butter, vanilla extract, ground cloves, and ginger until light and fluffy. Then, throw in the coconut flour, almond flour, and slivered almonds.
Continue mixing until it forms a soft dough. Cover and place in the refrigerator for 35 minutes. Meanwhile, preheat the air fryer to 315 degrees f.
Roll dough into small cookies and place them on the air fryer cake pan; gently press each cookie using the back of a spoon.
Bake these butter cookies for 13 minutes and serve.

NUTRITION:

Calories 94, Total Fat 3g, Saturated Fat 1g, Cholesterol 10mg, Sodium 92mg, Carbohydrates 15g, Fiber 1g, Sugars 7g, Protein 1g

BIRTHDAY CHOCOLATE RASPBERRY CAKE

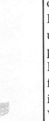

30 minutes	25 minutes	4

INGREDIENTS
1/3 cup monk fruit
1/4 cup unsalted butter, room temperature
1 egg plus 1 egg white, lightly whisked
3 ounces almond flour
2 tablespoons dutch-process cocoa powder
1/2 teaspoon ground cinnamon
1 tablespoon candied ginger
1/8 teaspoon table salt
For the filling:
2 ounces fresh raspberries
1/3 cup monk fruit
1 teaspoon fresh lime juice

DIRECTIONS:

Firstly, set your air fryer to cook at 315 degrees f. Then, spritz the inside of two cake pans with the butter-flavored cooking spray.
In a mixing bowl, beat the monk fruit and butter until creamy and uniform. Then, stir in the whisked eggs. Stir in the almond flour, cocoa powder, cinnamon, ginger and salt.
Press the batter into the cake pans; use a wide spatula to level the surface of the batter. Bake for 20 minutes or until a wooden stick inserted in the center of the cake comes out completely dry.
While your cake is baking, stir together all of the ingredients for the filling in a medium saucepan. Cook over high heat, stirring frequently and mashing with the back of a spoon; bring to a boil and decrease the temperature.
Continue to cook, stirring until the mixture thickens, for another 7 minutes. Let the filling cool to room temperature.
Spread 1/2 of raspberry filling over the first crust. Top with another crust; spread remaining filling over top. Spread frosting over top and sides of your cake.

NUTRITION:

Calories 440, Total Fat 16g, Saturated Fat 8g, Cholesterol 70mg, Sodium 240mg, Carbohydrates 58g, Fiber 1g, Sugars 48g, Protein 4g

OLD-FASHIONED MUFFINS

DIRECTIONS:

Grab two mixing bowls. In the first bowl, thoroughly combine the almond flour, baking powder, swerve, salt, anise, allspice and lemon zest. Take the second bowl; whisk coconut oil, sour cream, and eggs; whisk to combine well. Now, add the wet mixture to the dry mixture. Fold in the raspberries.
Press the batter mixture into a lightly greased muffin tin. Bake at 345 degrees for 15 minutes. Use a toothpick to check if your muffins are baked.

20 minutes	15 minutes	6

INGREDIENTS

1/2 cup raspberries
3/4 cup swerve
1/2 cup coconut oil
1 cup sour cream
1 ¼ teaspoons baking powder
2 cups almond flour
2 eggs
1/3 teaspoon ground allspice
1/3 teaspoon ground anise star
1/2 teaspoon grated lemon zest
1/4 teaspoon salt

NUTRITION:

Calories 300, Total Fat 10g, Saturated Fat 3g, Cholesterol 26mg, Sodium 350mg, Carbohydrates 47g, Fiber 2g, Sugars 19g,Protein 5g

DOUBLE CHOCOLATE WHISKEY BROWNIES

DIRECTIONS:

Microwave white chocolate and coconut oil until everything's melted; allow the mixture to cool at room temperature.
After that, thoroughly whisk the eggs, monk fruit, rum extract, cocoa powder and cardamom.
Next step, add the rum/egg mixture to the chocolate mixture. Stir in the flour and coconut flakes; mix to combine.
Mix cranberries with whiskey and let them soak for 15 minutes. Fold them into the batter. Press the batter into a lightly buttered cake pan. Air-fry for 35 minutes at 340 degrees f. Allow them to cool slightly on a wire rack before slicing and serving.

55 minutes	35 minutes	10

INGREDIENTS

3 tablespoons whiskey
8 ounces white chocolate
3/4 cup almond flour
1/4 cup coconut flakes
1/2 cup coconut oil
2 eggs plus an egg yolk, whisked
3/4 cup monk fruit
2 tablespoons cocoa powder, unsweetened
1/4 teaspoon ground cardamom
1 teaspoon pure rum extract

NUTRITION:

Calories 313, Total Fat 25g, Saturated Fat 6g, Cholesterol 78mg, Sodium 151mg, Carbohydrates 30g, Fiber 1g, Sugars 11g, Protein 4g

PICNIC BLACKBERRY MUFFINS

Directions:

In a mixing bowl, combine the almond flour, baking soda, baking powder, swerve, and salt. Whisk to combine well.
In another mixing bowl, mix the eggs, milk, coconut oil, and vanilla.
Now, add the wet egg mixture to dry the flour mixture. Then, carefully fold in the fresh blackberries; gently stir to combine.
Scrape the batter mixture into the muffin cups. Bake your muffins at 350 degrees f for 12 minutes or until the tops are golden brown.
Sprinkle some extra icing sugar over the top of each muffin if desired.
Serve

20 minutes	12 minutes	8

Ingredients
1 ½ cups almond flour
1/2 teaspoon baking soda
1 teaspoon baking powder
1/4 teaspoon kosher salt
1/2 cup swerve
2 eggs, whisked
1/2 cup milk
1/4 cup coconut oil, melted
1/2 teaspoon vanilla paste
1/2 cup fresh blackberries

Nutrition:

Calories 154, Total Fat 5g, Saturated Fat 1g, Cholesterol 19mg, Sodium 192mg, Carbohydrates 25g, Fiber 2g, Sugars 8g, Protein 3g

SUNDAY TART WITH WALNUTS

Directions:

Begin by preheating your air fryer to 360 degrees f. Spritz the sides and bottom of a baking pan with nonstick cooking spray.
Mix all ingredients until well combined. Scrape the batter into the prepared baking pan.
Bake approximately 13 minutes; use a toothpick to test for doneness and serve.

20 minutes	13 minutes	6

Ingredients
1 cup coconut milk
2 eggs
1/2 stick butter, at room temperature
1 teaspoon vanilla essence
1/4 teaspoon ground cardamom
1/4 teaspoon ground cloves
1/2 cup walnuts, ground
1/2 cup swerve
1/2 cup almond flour

Nutrition:

Calories 220, Total Fat 20g, Saturated Fat 7g, Cholesterol 60mg, Sodium 120mg, Carbohydrates 5g, Fiber 1g, Sugars 5g, Protein 5g

PEANUT BUTTER AND CHOCOLATE CHIP COOKIES

20 minutes | 11 minutes | 8

INGREDIENTS

1 stick butter, at room temperature
1 ¼ cups swerve
1/4 cup chunky peanut butter
1 teaspoon vanilla paste
1 fine almond flour
2/3 cup coconut flour
1/3 cup cocoa powder, unsweetened
1 ½ teaspoons baking powder
1/4 teaspoon ground cinnamon
1/4 teaspoon crystallized ginger
1/2 cup chocolate chips, unsweetened

DIRECTIONS:

In a mixing dish, beat the butter and swerve until creamy and uniform. Stir in the peanut butter and vanilla.
In another mixing dish, thoroughly combine the flour, cocoa powder, baking powder, cinnamon, and crystallized ginger.
Add the flour mixture to the peanut butter mixture; mix to combine well. Afterwards, fold in the chocolate chips.
Drop by large spoonfuls onto a parchment-lined air fryer basket. Bake at 365 degrees f for 11 minutes or until golden brown on the top and serve.

NUTRITION:

Calories 303, Total Fat 28g, Saturated Fat 6g, Cholesterol 98mg, Sodium 251mg, Carbohydrates 10g, Fiber 4g, Sugars 7g, Protein 6g

Conclusion

I am extremely glad and happy that you were able to go through the whole book. I sincerely hope that you enjoyed the contents of the book and found it useful.
The next step from here is to explore even further and find your own culinary footing! Learn the basics from these recipes, and come up with your very own awesome Ninja Foodi recipes!
I wish you luck in your future ventures and hope that you stay safe and healthy.
Stay tuned for more books available soon!

Hannah.

CPSIA information can be obtained
at www.ICGtesting.com
Printed in the USA
LVHW061412131120
671374LV00011B/703

9 781914 069192